MORE THAN
A TREATMENT

*How To Create Exceptional
Experiences That Increase
Patient Satisfaction And Improve
Treatment Outcomes*

Dr. East Phillips, DAOM, L.Ac.

INDIE BOOKS
INTERNATIONAL

With admiration, respect, and much love, I dedicate this book to my fellow practitioners in healthcare.

CONTENTS

PREFACE

What you are about to read comes straight from my heart.

I want your patients to heal, feel better, and live joyful and fulfilling lives.

I also want the same for you.

I want you to have a genuine passion for what you contribute to the health and well-being of your patients. I want you to sustain that passion throughout your time in practice, and enjoy fond memories and a legacy of helping others in the years afterward.

I want you to feel the thrill of success and to be beyond satisfied with your choice to pursue a career in healthcare. I also want you to live an abundantly prosperous and gratifying life.

The tools and ideas presented in this book can help you achieve all of this.

PART I

Why Create An Exceptional Experience?

At the end of the day, people won't remember what you said or did, they will remember how you made them feel.

—MAYA ANGELOU

This applies to your treatments, as well.

There really is a difference between merely delivering a treatment and providing your patients with an exceptional experience.

The latter undoubtedly results in our patients feeling and getting better.

After all, isn't that the goal?

CHAPTER 1

An Urgent Call For Increased Patient Satisfaction

This is a tale of two treatments. Treatment number one took place at a high-end day spa circa 2002.

For years, my office was next to a fancy, modern, and luxurious day spa. I often saw women lounging around in robes, fluffy slippers, and eye masks, getting thoroughly pampered. I not only wanted that—I needed that. I was feeling burned out, and seeing these ladies pampered every day made me want it even more.

With school debt from Chinese medical school totaling over $80,000 and a high cost of living in San Diego, it took me nearly two years to save up the $299 for a spoil-yourself-package at the fancy spa.

When I was finally able to book my package, I was so excited to treat myself. I was feeling drained from seeing twenty-five to thirty patients per week in my private practice, holding another part-time job in the fitness industry, and dealing with the everyday stresses of life.

I checked in with the receptionist and waited in the tranquil, aromatherapy-filled waiting room. "*Ahhh*. Rest and relaxation," I thought to myself.

Then my name was called. "East?" the therapist said.

My heart fluttered in anticipation of receiving the same kind of pampering and nurturing that I had given to my patients for the previous six years (four years in school and two in practice). I really needed this.

As we walked down the dimly-lit hallway to my treatment room, the therapist and I exchanged some small talk.

"Is this your first time at the spa?" my therapist asked.

"Yes, it is. I'm so excited."

No response from the therapist.

"How is your day going so far?" I asked.

"Good, good," she replied curtly.

"Have you worked here long?"

"No." I sensed either she didn't like working there or she didn't want to engage in small talk.

"How long have you been a massage therapist?" I asked.

"Six months," she replied.

"That's great. How do you like it?" I inquired.

"Actually, I hate it," she said as she looked back at me and gave me a look that seemed to say, "OK, are you happy now? Enough with the questions."

My dancing heart fell flat on the floor. *Ouch.*

To this day, nearly twenty years later, that was one of the worst massage/treatment experiences of my life. This girl's massage therapy not only wasn't therapeutic, it reflected her attitude toward her chosen profession, and my $299 would have been better spent elsewhere. In fact, I felt ten times worse after my session with her. It was as though I somehow took on her negative energy. It took me a long time to wash myself of that dismal experience (insert emoji of disappointed face with tears streaming from sad eyes).

Treatment number two took place in a small, private office in the gorgeous coastal town of La Jolla. Before my session with this amazing woman, I had heard rumors about a practitioner of Chinese medicine named MJ, who had special skills passed down to her from her grandfather, a highly skilled and dearly revered Korean healer. She charged $300 for a one-hour treatment. "Wow! What does she do that is worth $300?" I remember thinking to myself. I wanted to find out, so I scheduled an appointment with her.

To this day, that treatment remains the most incredible acupuncture experience I have received. Everything about the session, from the initial phone call to the follow-up, was impeccable.

I scheduled with her via a phone call. During this initial conversation, she set some expectations around the treatment.

First, she asked me to be punctual, informing me that she is always on time and never runs late. The appointment would be fifty-five minutes. No shorter. No longer.

Also, she advised me to schedule the appointment so I could go directly home after the treatment and not stop for food, gas, or to meet with anyone else afterward. She explained that for me to get the most significant benefit from our session together, I would need to follow her directions.

I arrived a few minutes early to my appointment. MJ was waiting for me at the entrance to her office. She stood at the open door, which led to her office. MJ was impeccably coifed with her long black hair pulled back in a stylish bun. She wore single pearl earrings and a simple strand of pearls around her neck. No other jewelry.

She was wearing a beautifully tailored, modern-style lab coat over a black dress that was hemmed about two inches below her knees, with patent-leather flats.

Everything about her body language said "Welcome," and she exuded a sense of warmth and caring with a big, genuine smile. As we walked in together, she led me into her treatment office, softly guiding me by touching my shoulder in a comforting, reassuring manner.

Her treatment office was immaculate; clean, very Zen-like, with minimal decorations. In her reception area, she had a small desk where she sat on one side, and I sat across from her. She asked me questions regarding my health and what I wanted to get out of the treatment. When I talked, she listened intently. She held such a deep space for me and my healing. I have not felt this from any other practitioner. At times it seemed as though she could see through me. No judgment. No scolding. Just a profound sense of listening from her heart.

When she took me back to the treatment room, it was just as Zen and perfectly kept as the rest of her office. The treatment table was extra-large and extra-luxurious. She used the most comfortable, soft, thick sheets, and lying on her table, I felt as if I were floating on warm clouds. There was a faint hint of music in the background. It sounded a bit like healing bowls or chimes. It smelled *clean*, if that makes sense. I asked her several questions, to which she smiled and replied, "No questions, please. Just relax and receive." This allowed me to get really enveloped in the treatment.

She began my treatment with me lying face-up on her table. Then she had me roll over. She finished by having me roll back over to lie face-up again. She may have worked on me for forty minutes, but it felt like days. Time seemed to warp and slow down. I didn't feel the insertion of one single needle or hear the tearing open of any needle packages. Was she even using needles? Yes, she was. I know this because periodically I peeked out from my closed eyes to see. I just didn't feel the usual slight stick of a needle. I did, however, feel the energy move in my body as she worked on me. I felt all the stress and tension in my body release and a deep sense of inner peace, balance, and calm that is difficult to explain with words.

After the treatment, she allowed me to take my time getting up and reacclimate to the surroundings. Handing me a cup of tea, she walked me out of her office and told me she would call me the next day to check in on me. I followed her instructions and went straight home. I journaled that night, and it was as though many things became clear to me.

As promised, MJ called me the next day. She asked me how I was feeling and if I had any questions. We talked for a little while, and without hesitating, I booked a second session with her right there on the phone.

After that experience with MJ, I immediately implemented several things into my own practice. I cleared out all clutter and organized my supplies into little compartments away from lines of sight. I hired a *feng shui* consultant to provide me with ways to effectively create a healing and serene ambiance in my office and treatment space. I stopped using table paper and bought high-quality linens. I started wearing a beautifully tailored lab coat. I went from multiple treatment rooms to just one and worked with one patient at a time. I sat with each patient before each treatment and took the time to talk first. These things are still part of my practice today, nearly ten years later.

If these experiences represent two polar opposites of a scale, where do you think your treatments sit? Are you grumpy and complaining? Are you pleasant, energized, and fully present? Do you give robot-like, protocol-centered treatments while your mind is somewhere entirely different? Do you give your patients an experience that leaves them feeling genuinely cared for and better than when they first arrived? Is it your intention to provide exceptional experiences?

Perhaps it should be, and here's why.

Providing exceptional treatment experiences will:

- Increase patient satisfaction
- Increase treatment outcomes
- Result in patient retention and referrals
- Allow you to charge more for your treatments

As healthcare providers, we are very familiar with objective measurement scales. One of the most commonly used scales is the visual analog scale (VAS), through which we have patients rate their pain on a scale from zero to ten (0 – 10), with zero indicating no pain and ten representing unbearable sensations.

But what if the scale that measures the patient experience actually goes from *negative ten* to ten (-10 – 10), with zero in the middle? Haven't you ever experienced a session from someone that you would say is subpar? Look at this scale and think to yourself: Where do you think your patients would rate your treatments on this scale? Would you like your ratings to be farther to the right, closer to exceptional? Read on, and I'll provide you with ways to accomplish just that.

TREATMENT EXPERIENCE SCALE

–10	–5	0	5	10
Ghastly	Subpar	Unremarkable	Average	Exceptional

CHAPTER 2

Bringing Magic Back To Medicine

My parents named me East in the '70s. You would think with a name like that, I would most certainly go straight into East Asian medicine. However, that was not the case. In fact, I was actually heading toward a western medical school before I found my way.

After receiving a bachelor's degree in business and realizing I didn't want any job I could see in the business world, I had made up my mind that I wanted to devote my life to helping others. I was taking prerequisites at the University of California San Diego (UC San Diego), studying for the MCAT and working a full-time project management job during the day. I was pretty busy. My free time consisted of exercise and a new love for the practice of yoga.

As fate would have it, one of the students in my small, seven-person yoga class was a physician and professor at UC San Diego Medical School. We often talked after our weekly yoga class about medicine and my longing to join the ranks of physicians, hopefully after being accepted to UC San Diego. I think my physician friend sensed early on that my interest in medicine was more natural or alternative.

One night after yoga, she suggested that I visit the local school for alternative medicine.

"What kind of a college is it?" I asked.

"It is a school for Chinese medicine," she replied.

"You mean acupuncture?" I said with a twisted look of torture on my face.

"It's more than just acupuncture," she said.

"There is no way. I hate needles."

"East, trust me. Before you spend seven years of your life heading in the direction of Western medicine only to finally realize you are more alternative, you might want to go straight into a natural form of medicine."

"But it's *needles*. The only thing I know about Chinese culture is Chinese food," I said.

"Just go check it out. What can it hurt?"

The next day, I took her advice. I left work a little early and ventured into the school's admissions office.

"Hi. I'm interested in your programs here," I said to the receptionist.

"Great," she replied, with a warm, friendly smile on her face. "The best person for you to talk to is Elaine, our admissions officer. Let me see if she can talk to you right now." She picked up the phone to call Elaine.

"No, that's OK, there's no reason to bother her. I can take home some information," I quickly answered.

"Not a problem at all," the helpful receptionist said, as she waited for Elaine to answer. Then, "Elaine, there's someone here. Uh, wait; Hun, what's your name?"

"My name is East."

"I love that," she replied.

"Um, East is here and has some questions regarding our school. Can you talk to her?"

She hung up the phone.

"Elaine would love to talk with you. Her office is through that door."

Gulp. "This is getting a little too serious. I'm just curious here," I thought.

Elaine opened the door before I could even get there and welcomed me in with a big, warm-hearted smile and handshake. "Hi, I'm the admissions officer here at Pacific College of Oriental Medicine. What questions do you have about our programs?"

"I don't really know anything about them, actually. A doctor friend of mine suggested I come and take a look at your school to see if it's what I'm looking for. I'm on track to go to medical school—hopefully at UC San Diego," I told her.

"Wow, OK. It's so great that your friend sent you here. I'll tell you what; in about thirty minutes, one of the founders of our school is teaching a class on the foundations of Chinese medicine. That would be a great class for you to sit in on. What do you think? Do you have the time?" she asked.

"I guess so. What room?" I asked.

She directed me to the room, which was a brief walk across the campus.

As I walked to the classroom, I looked around the campus, taking in all the rather unusual symbols, Chinese characters, and instructional posters, many of which looked like ancient scrolls. I walked past the school's clinic, where huge glass windows look into the herb room. I remember thinking how incredibly fascinating it all was. It felt as if I were being exposed to ancient secrets: natural methods for healing. There was a sense of mysticism and magic. I saw hundreds of jars with grasses, seeds, sticks, and twigs in them. These were used for healing? Just touring the school in those thirty minutes, I became more and more intrigued.

I sat in on that fateful class, and my life changed forever.

Fortuitously, the professor for this class was Alex Tiberi, one of the founders of the Pacific College of Oriental Medicine (PCOM) and a most revered professor, practitioner, mentor, and an amazing all-around individual.

There he stood in jeans, hiking boots, and a long-sleeved, cowboy-style, button-down with a vest on top. He pushed his black, wildly curly hair away from his face as he talked with great animation and enthusiasm. Tattoos of roses, intriguing Tibetan symbols, and other mythical images coming up both forearms seemed to tell their own stories of adventure and ancient knowledge. As Alex spoke, his huge smile radiated as if straight from his heart. His eyes had a sparkle that matched his playful, childlike manner. He spoke of the foundations of Chinese medicine as if he were telling us the most coveted secrets of all time. He was almost like a yin and yang symbol incarnate, all yang masculine energy with a simultaneous, gentle, nurturing, yin-like energy. He both whispered and spoke loudly of the many secrets passed down to him from his teachers and mentors. To me, and probably many others, he was Chinese medicine come to life.

As he presented his lecture, I was glued. I didn't stay for thirty minutes. I remained for an hour-and-a-half and left at the first break.

The very next day, I called Elaine and told her I wanted to take steps to apply. She said it was too late to join the next cohort, which began in one week, and that I would have to wait a semester. I told her I would do anything to join the upcoming group. She told me I would have to get transcripts from all my previous schools, fill out a lengthy application, and complete an entrance interview with her—all within two days. I told her I would see her in two days for my interview with all the required paperwork in hand.

I took the next day off work and gathered up all the documents. I waited in long lines to get transcripts from my undergraduate school and stayed up very late filling out lengthy, thorough, and thought-provoking entrance paperwork, which included an essay about why I wanted to attend PCOM.

As promised, I got all the documents to Elaine and a mere two days later, sat down for my entrance interview. I still remember the excitement I felt to be drawn so strongly toward something. I felt as if I had found my calling, my purpose. I had found my people.

Elaine asked me a series of entrance questions, but one stands out to this day: "Are you sure you want to do this?" Was I? How could I be? I hadn't even known this school existed a week prior.

I remember looking at Elaine and saying, "Honestly, I don't know, but I have to do this. I feel so strongly about this that I have to see it through."

I wonder what she thought, all those years ago.

I have never looked back.

I have never once regretted my decision.

I absolutely loved learning about Chinese medicine and the many ancient and natural ways to help others.

Alex had the same passion, enthusiasm, and way of providing treatments. He taught several classes during our four-year master's program and repeatedly stressed to us that the most essential thing in giving a treatment is providing the patient with an exceptional, almost magical experience.

"Instead of just cupping your patients like this," he would say, demonstrating a robot-like manner, "give your patients 'fire cupping!'" He said this dramatically, his arms moving about wildly, voice raised, a large flame traveling from a hemostat holding an alcohol-saturated cotton ball into a glass cup.

Alex always stressed the importance of holding a sacred healing space for the patient—even more than getting the specific acupuncture points right or herbal formulas correct. He encouraged us to bring a sense of magic and mysticism into our medical practice. He believed that if we did so, our patients would heal and get better, faster.

It's interesting that modern medicine is now embracing what Alex always knew and taught us all along. Studies have shown that patients with greater satisfaction after a health-related session obtain better treatment outcomes.[1] Happier and more satisfied patients undoubtedly return and refer their family and friends. With more positive treatment outcomes and enhanced treatment experiences, patients (and insurance companies, in some cases) are willing to pay more for sessions. More patients, plus the ability to charge more for services, equals more money for you. Win-win.

[1] Manary, Matthew P., William Boulding, Richard Staelin, and Seth W. Glickman. "The Patient Experience and Health Outcomes." *New England Journal of Medicine* 368, no. 3 (2013): 201–3. https://doi.org/10.1056/nejmp1211775.

Alex's influence on me and the way I approach the art of patient care was deep and profound. It has also carried into my own teaching style over the nearly fifteen years of teaching Chinese medicine to hundreds of emerging acupuncturists. I have strived to pass on Alex's genuine passion for healing others and provide them with exceptional experiences rather than just delivering average treatments.

I have immense gratitude, respect, and admiration for Alex Tiberi. He was the guide who led me to find my purpose and true passion. His influence in complementary and alternative medicine runs deep and wide. I am not the only one who was moved and inspired by him. Thousands were touched by his presence while he walked the Earth, and thousands continue to be influenced by the legacy he left behind with his passing: patients, students, fellow healthcare practitioners, his loved ones, and all the lives touched by his contribution to healthcare and the art of practice.

I use the word *art* with purpose because I believe the practice of helping others really is an art. This notion is something I feel is lost to many modern practitioners. Too many patients, not aligned with their true passions, too much focus on the treatment versus the experience of the patient: all are reasons for being led away from the altruistic drive to have a genuine, positive impact on the lives of others.

With nearly twenty years of practice behind me, I absolutely know that when I approach my practice from a desire to create an exceptional experience for my patients, rather than just to deliver a treatment, an entirely magical world opens up to me. I would *love* for each and every one of us to provide exceptional treatment experiences because I believe the benefits are far-reaching. These include:

- Patients get better faster with improved treatment outcomes.

- Data and word-of-mouth will reveal a higher efficacy of our medicine, thereby attracting more patients and integration with other healthcare practitioners.

- Job satisfaction increases.

- Patients are willing to pay more for your services.

PART II

The Four Stops On The Road To An Exceptional Experience

If you want patients who are more than just satisfied—they are delighted, with improved treatment outcomes—or you want to build more wealth for yourself and maintain enthusiasm for what you do, then join me on a little road trip.

Our journey will include four stops along the way.

Each stop will contain patient satisfaction secrets that you can incorporate into your practice to transform your treatments into exceptional experiences for your patients.

CHAPTER 3

Our First Stop:
The Golden Circle

The *Golden Circle* represents your entire treatment process—from a warm invitation, through the scheduling process, to a welcome from your office staff, to follow-up and a continuous connection with the patient.

What if we got rid of the "treat 'em and street 'em" mentality that seems to be the norm in healthcare today and treated our patients like our most revered loved ones? Imagine what that would look and feel like for you and your patients. Isn't that how you would like to be treated?

WARM INVITATION

Let's say you are out and about in the world—be it a social or networking event or just in your everyday life. Someone asks something like, "What do you do for a living?" What do you say? Do you tell them the type of healthcare professional you are and then leave it at that, or do you invite them into more dialogue?

When you tell people that you have a particular type of practice (for example, acupuncture, chiropractic, naturopathic, Reiki, Healing Touch, boutique medical practice, massage therapy, etc.), what else would you add? Are the sentences that follow anything like these?

- Have you had acupuncture/chiropractic/naturopathy/ massage before?

- Would you like to come in for a session with me?

- I would *love* to treat you.

"I'd love to treat you." What a warm invitation. Wouldn't you, yourself, want to be treated by someone who shows that kind of passion and enthusiasm for what they do? Your high levels of energy and excitement may be the catalyst for someone wanting to try your specific modality.

This reminds me of a time years ago when I attended an indoor cycling training workshop. The master cycling teacher played a Britney Spears song. "Yuck," I thought. "I hate Britney Spears music. This is going to be awful." That cycling teacher was so over-the-top enthusiastic about that song, however, that I caught his enthusiasm and not only bought the Britney Spears song he played during the training, I purchased two others. Our energy and passion are contagious, and people are drawn to them like moths to a flame.

Barbara was a conscientious healthcare professional, a highly skilled practitioner in Southern California.[2] She was experiencing a challenge: not enough new patients to generate a thriving practice.

Barbara came to me to help her attract more patients. After asking her some questions, I determined that she was attending the right networking events and performing the correct practice-building efforts, such as handing out cards at Chamber of Commerce events, business networking and speaking opportunities. Yet no one was making an appointment to come to see her for treatments.

"When you are at these events, and you tell them you are an acupuncturist, where does the conversation go from there?" I asked.

"Well, that's it. I hand them my card and move on."

"Why don't you invite them to come in for treatment?" I asked.

"Because I don't want to come across as salesy," Barbara replied.

"I promise you that a warm and genuine invitation to be treated is not salesy at all," I assured her. "In fact, it is refreshing and creates

---

[2] True story, but names and details have been changed to protect confidentiality.

a connection. Your enthusiasm and genuine passion for wanting to help people will leave them wanting more information or more time with you. The next time someone asks you, 'What do you do for a living,' let that person know that you are an acupuncturist and you would love to treat them."

"Oh, I couldn't do that. It would be too pushy," said Barbara.

"Yes, you can. And it isn't pushy," I replied. "It is showing that you are passionate about what you do and you care about the person you're talking to. Wouldn't you want to be treated by someone with high enthusiasm and passion for what they do?"

I continued. "You can hand someone a card and say, as you look them in the eyes, 'I'd love to treat you. Come see me.' You can even schedule their appointment right then and there if the conversation goes in that direction."

It wasn't easy for Barbara, but she said she would try.

At the next networking event, she was nervous to try my suggestion, but she overcame her fears. She extended a warm invitation for a treatment to everyone she met. To her surprise, she booked three new patient appointments. An added bonus: Those new patients shared with their friends that they had found an exceptional and genuinely passionate acupuncturist who really cared about her patients, resulting in even *more* new patients.

Barbara's new way of looking at how to attract patients to her practice paid big dividends. That little tweak helped her double her practice.

Ease Of Scheduling

Speaking of scheduling an appointment with you—how easy is it for a patient to make an appointment? Do you offer online scheduling, or do you play phone tag for days with patients? I believe that healing begins when a patient makes an appointment with a healthcare provider because the appointment signals the intention to get well.

If patients have finally reached a state in which they are committed to getting better, and they cannot schedule with you at that exact moment, they may not ever schedule at all. They leave that state of intention, and the moment is lost. They may wake up the next morning and not feel as motivated as they did before.

If online scheduling isn't possible or realistic for you, at the very least have someone available to receive scheduling calls for you. It may seem silly, but even something as seemingly small as the ease (or difficulty) of scheduling affects the overall patient experience. Remember the Golden Rule: If you, yourself, really wanted to get better and were having a difficult time scheduling an appointment with someone, how would you feel?

Another experience enhancement related to ease-of-scheduling is to send email or text appointment reminders to your patients. If you have this capability, do it. Many office systems or electronic health record programs feature automated functions that do this for you; your patients will feel that much more taken care of and will appreciate the added reminder.

OFFICE STAFF

Any and all office personnel who engage with patients are part of the overall treatment experience. Make sure that they are pleasant, warm, compassionate, and demonstrate genuine care for your patients, just like you. I have experienced both scenarios.

I once worked at a wellness center where our receptionist was *adored* by our patients. They brought her flowers and gifts. They loved her, and she loved them. Patients frequently told me they looked forward to coming to the office knowing that our receptionist would welcome them with her big smile and even a hug from time to time. She was part of the experience and definitely part of the favorable treatment outcomes we established.

Conversely, I was part of another wellness center where the receptionist complained about every one of the doctors for things like running late, not giving her a treatment, not buying lunch for the office, or not letting everyone leave early on Fridays. She even snapped at patients for being late or "too early." It got so bad that some patients started to schedule their appointments on the days they knew she was not going to be there. I even learned that some of our patients were so repelled by that receptionist, they went to the wellness center up the street where another colleague worked instead.

Be it negative or positive, our staff members have an influence over our patients. Make sure that interaction is a positive one, or it could undo the progress you are making with your patients. Less-than-stellar staff can potentially jeopardize your entire relationship with a patient.

TIMELINESS

Start on time. End on time. Period.

Punctuality shows respect for the patient as a person. Research into what drives patient satisfaction has found that one of the most significant factors for dissatisfaction is long wait times.[3] How do you feel when you have to wait to be seen by a practitioner? Do you like it when the scheduled treatment time goes over, and now you run late the rest of your day?

---

[3] Prakash, Bhanu. "Patient Satisfaction." *Journal of Cutaneous and Aesthetic Surgery* 3, no. 3 (2010): 151. https://doi.org/10.4103/0974-2077.74491.

If the nature of your practice makes timeliness nearly impossible, then at minimum, consider incorporating the following three strategies to lessen a patient's dissatisfaction with waiting:

Adjust expectations. If you tend to run late, let your patients know this. Inform them that you sometimes run late and that the *longest* they will wait is [X] minutes. That way, they can be prepared and maybe even bring something productive (other than their phones) to occupy their time while they wait.

Spend more one-on-one time with the patient. Research has shown that while patients satisfaction levels decrease with extended wait times, the satisfaction levels will rise when the doctor spends more one-on-one time with the patient.[4]

Occupy their time. Provide something in your waiting room other than, or in addition to, medical office norms (the latest issue of *People* or *The View* on the television). Here are some unique ideas for waiting room activities:

- Offer **coloring.** Coloring books have been proven to reduce stress and anxiety. Specifically, coloring preprinted designs or mandalas has been found to be significantly

---

[4] Anderson, Roger T, Fabian T Camacho, and Rajesh Balkrishnan. "Willing to Wait?: The Influence of Patient Wait Time on Satisfaction with Primary Care." *BMC Health Services Research*, 7:31 (2007). https://doi.org/10.1186/1472-6963-7-31.

more effective than coloring a blank page.[5] Maybe it is the rhythmic motions of the repeating patterns in mandalas, or not having to decide what to draw or where to draw that helps keep the mind at peace and allow for the reduction of anxiety and the increase in relaxation. In any event, the suggestion is to make pages with preprinted images or patterns available on which people can color and be creative.

• Pass time with **jigsaw puzzles.** Many people enjoy jigsaw puzzles, and research suggests that engaging in them distorts the sense of time.[6] This means that if you are running late by fifteen or twenty minutes and they are playing with the jigsaw puzzles in your waiting room, they may think they waited five or ten minutes.

• Make **crossword puzzle books** available.

• Provide a **Zen garden** with sand and rocks.

• Lay out a variety of **coffee table interest books.**

---

[5] Drake, Crystal R., H. Russell Searight, and Kristina Olson-Pupek. "The Influence of Art-Making on Negative Mood States in University Students." *American Journal of Applied Psychology.* Science and Education Publishing, January 23, 2014. http://pubs.sciepub.com/ajap/2/3/3/.

[6] Iwamoto, Yuko, and Minoru Hoshiyama. "Alteration of Time Perception in Young and Elderly People during Jigsaw Puzzle Tasks with Different Complexities." *Occupational Therapy International* 18, no. 4 (2011): 194–200. https://doi.org/10.1002/oti.322.

Make sure to regularly discard old magazines and clean the items in your waiting rooms. Magazines and objects played with by numerous people have been shown to carry bacteria and other harmful germs.[7]

ESTABLISHING PATIENT-CENTERED EXPECTATIONS

Clearly define and set expectations, with feedback from your patients. If you believe the treatment plan consists of six weeks, ask the patient if anything coming up in the weeks ahead may get in the way.

More than ever before, patients today want to feel as though they have a say in their healthcare. If it is imperative that they follow your treatment plan, then explain it to them in detail until they fully understand and commit to comply. Do not assume that they will adhere to your instructions just because you say so. Get their agreement. Ask questions; give information. Take the time to set the stage right from the beginning. As the adage goes: Measure twice, cut once.

---

[7] Charnock, Colin. "Swabbing of Waiting Room Magazines Reveals Only Low Levels of Bacterial Contamination." The British journal of general practice : the journal of the Royal College of General Practitioners. Oxford University Press, January 1, 2005. https://www.ncbi.nlm.nih.gov/pmc/articles/PMC1266241/.

INVOLVE FAMILY MEMBERS, CARETAKERS AND/OR LOVED ONES

Patient satisfaction surveys have revealed that patients want to have their family members actively involved in the decision process as well.[8] This makes perfect sense because most likely, your patient's condition is also affecting family members, caretakers and/or loved ones. When delivering a treatment plan and obtaining consent and agreement from the patient, involve an immediate family member as well. Invite the spouse, partner, mother, father, child, sister, roommate, or other loved one into the treatment session.

If having a family member or loved one present during the treatment plan conversation isn't possible, you can provide handouts for these people so they feel included. Consider a checklist of what to look for or how they can help to contribute to a positive treatment outcome; perhaps a handout explaining the condition and the potential effects it may have on a family unit. Interestingly, the idea of involving family members in a patient's healthcare is not a new concept. In fact, it is included in the Hippocratic Oath.

---

[8] Bogner, Jennifer, Erinn M Hade, Juan Peng, Cynthia L Beaulieu, Susan D Horn, John D Corrigan, Flora M Hammond, et al. "Family Involvement in Traumatic Brain Injury Inpatient Rehabilitation: A Propensity Score Analysis of Effects on Outcomes During the First Year After Discharge." Archives of Physical Medicine and Rehabilitation. U.S. National Library of Medicine, May 9, 2019. https://www.ncbi.nlm.nih.gov/pubmed/31077646.

I will remember that I do not treat a fever chart, a cancerous growth, but a sick human being, whose illness may affect the person's family and economic stability. My responsibility includes these related problems, if I am to care adequately for the sick.

Follow Up During Treatment Plan and After

Going full circle (pun intended), do you follow up with all your patients to see how they are doing throughout the treatment plan cycle as well as after treatment has ended?

If you prescribe herbs, supplements, medications, or lifestyle advice, do you follow up throughout the treatment plan period to see if the patient has questions, and/or is complying? Personally, I've prescribed herbs to patients and later learned because they were unsure of the proper preparation method, they didn't take them. Then, after a week, when they returned for treatment, they explained why they didn't comply. Patients don't always call or email to ask questions. If only I had called (or had an assistant call) to make sure they were taking their herbs, we wouldn't have lost a whole week in their healing process.

Do you keep your patients within the *Golden Circle* by following up with each and every one of them—even those you may have referred out to someone else or those who have completed their treatment plan with you?

I like to start my follow-up communication with words like, "I've been thinking about you." Or, "I came across this research and wanted to pass it along to you because you immediately came to my mind when I was reading it."

Just like the warm invitation, personal communication that seems to come from your heart will go a long way with patients in making them feel genuinely cared for and special.

An added bonus to following up with your patient post-treatment is an ability to collect additional data on the efficacy of the services you provide. Staff did this very effectively at the Chopra Center, where I acted as the staff acupuncturist for some time. Six months after completing a wellness retreat, attendees would receive a survey ascertaining post-treatment effects and compliance. Survey responses provided the center with incredible insight into the efficacy and sustainability of their programs.

What if you knew that six, nine, or even twelve months after a treatment plan with you, your patients were still on track and feeling well? With a "treat 'em and street 'em" approach we really never know the impact we have on others or how we may improve our services.

Another benefit of following up with patients after a treatment plan cycle has ended is that it allows you an easy way of obtaining patient testimonials. Here is an example of an email dialogue.

You: "Good morning Joe, I am emailing you to follow up and see how you are feeling."

Patient Joe: "I feel amazing! Your treatment was really incredible, and I had no idea I could feel this good again after just one session. I had the best sleep I've had in years last night. I have been pain-free ever since I left your office."

You: "That's so great to hear. Thank you for sharing that with me. May I use that as a testimonial?"

This is natural, organic, and easier than asking patients and/or clients to take time out of their already hectic and busy schedules to sit down and write us a testimonial.

Patient Care Comanagement

Do you discuss your patients' care with other providers with whom they are receiving treatment? If not, why not? What if we took a team approach to our patients' well-being? Think of how powerful that would be.

Working with other healthcare practitioners helps us widen our understandings and experiences and offers the best of all worlds to our patients. Wouldn't you want to be offered all possible approaches to your healthcare, from natural to traditional standards of care? What if you had a team of physicians who worked together to provide you with the best possible care? Perhaps a natural approach can solve the problem and prevent surgery. Maybe your condition is too severe for a natural remedy, and a more aggressive intervention is required. Having a team of healthcare providers from all corners offers our patients, and ourselves, the best possible treatments.

The Chopra Center, located in San Diego, California, already mentioned above, not only models excellent patient care comanagement but also remains one of the highest examples of what it means to provide an exceptional patient experience. I had the incredible privilege of working at the Center for some time, acting as the lead acupuncturist in the Mind-Body Medical Group. This group of highly respected and experienced practitioners provides integrated care to the guests and patients who visit the center from all over the world.

> *While the Chopra Center is centered around the healing*
> *philosophies and principles of Ayurvedic medicine,*
> *it welcomes other practitioners to join the team and*
> *provide a holistic team approach to solving the health*
> *concerns of their guests. I will talk more about the*
> *Chopra Center at to our next stop: The Healing Temple.*

In addition, working as a team and reaching out to other healthcare providers working with our patients provides us the opportunity to get the entire story when our patient may not be willing or able to fill in the gaps.

I once had a patient who wanted to wean off her antidepressant medications. I told her I would work with her as long as I could discuss her desires with her primary physician, who had prescribed the drugs. She agreed. When I spoke with her physician, I was informed of two suicide attempts that she had failed to mention to me in our hour-and-a-half initial intake. Understandably, her physician was very hesitant to lower the dosage of her antidepressants. Together, however, we came up with a treatment plan that very slowly weaned her from her medications while closely monitoring the patient. This comanagement process made us both feel more comfortable. Weaning the patient off medications didn't happen as quickly as the patient initially wanted, but we all—myself, the prescribing physician, and the patient—bought into the treatment plan.

It is essential that we do not work in a bubble. We do not know it all, and our patients don't always give us all the information. Working as an integrative healthcare team allows us to catch each other's blind spots and, indeed, give our patients comprehensive health care.

One organization promoting this type of collaborate and truly integrative approach is the Academy of Integrative Health & Medicine (AIHM). They are led by a powerhouse team of physicians and healthcare practitioners who understand the impact of joining forces and working together toward the common goal of providing exceptional patient care. I would recommend becoming a member of this organization as a way of staying current on the newest trends in healthcare and learning about other practices. See for yourself—here are their mission and vision statements.

Mission of AIHM

The Academy of Integrative Health & Medicine is dedicated to engaging a global community of health professionals and health seekers in innovative education, leadership, interprofessional collaboration, research and advocacy that embraces all global healing traditions, to promote the creation of health and the delivery of evidence-informed comprehensive, affordable, sustainable person-centered care.

Vision of AIHM

We envision a world where humanity and the planet are healthy.

We, too have a dream.

Where healthcare is about health and available to all.

Where prevention is our foundation and mechanical fixes are embraced when we need them.

Where all healthcare providers work collaboratively to heal body, mind and spirit.

Where sustainability is integrated into our culture, practice and training.

Working together to establish a new paradigm of health care for humanity and the planet.

We are the solution.[9]

---

[9] https://www.aihm.org/

None of us is the end-all, be-all in healthcare. We all play a role in bringing a patient to a breakthrough.

Think of a jar with a really stubborn lid that will not open. You try with all your strength to twist, but to no avail. You cannot.

You hand the jar to a friend. The friend tries mightily to open it. Nope.

After another four attempts from other strong, capable people, a small child walks up and says, "Let me try." With very little effort at all, that child opens that jar right up—*POP*.

Was that child gifted with superhuman strength? No, not at all. Rather, everyone before him loosened that jar lid ever so slightly. The breakthrough simply happened when the small child tried.

All of us contribute to our patients' getting well. Sometimes we are there for the breakthrough; sometimes we are not. Regardless, we are helping in some way, and it almost always takes a number of us to deliver our patients to their desired breakthrough.

Thank-You-For-Your-Referral System

Two heads are better than one—isn't that how the saying goes? In healthcare, having a team of practitioners is undoubtedly the best approach to providing the patient with the most comprehensive care.

Most of us have gone to school for thousands of hours and engaged in years of clinical experience. It is nearly impossible for us to know about all the different healthcare practices that are out there. We can, however, educate each other on our areas of specialty within healthcare so that we may understand all that is available for our patients.

Here is an easy way of teaching other practitioners what we do while increasing our referrals: Thank-You-For-Your-Referral Letters.

Years ago, a physical therapist (PT) whom I did not personally know referred to me a severe case of frozen shoulder. While I had never met this particular PT, he had heard about me from a colleague and told the patient to try acupuncture as a last resort before possibly seeking surgery. "It's worth a try," he told the patient.

I treated the patient once a week for four weeks with acupuncture, heat therapy, and a modality called *gua sha*. After the four weeks, the patient was ultimately pain-free and gained full range of motion in the affected shoulder.

I wrote up a brief and professional "Thank You For Your Referral," a letter summarizing the treatment plan and the outcome I had realized with this frozen shoulder patient. In addition, I attached some current literature on the efficacy of acupuncture in treating frozen shoulder and other shoulder-related injuries. I then drove over to the PT's office, introduced myself to the referring PT, and personally delivered the Thank-You-For-Your-Referral Letter.

The PT's mouth dropped open as he read my letter. "Are you kidding me? That guy's shoulder was completely frozen. You mean to tell me that after just four weekly sessions with you, his shoulder is 100 percent? What did you do? I had no idea acupuncture could do that."

I shared with him all that I had done with the patient and the current findings on the efficacy of acupuncture on shoulder issues. I thanked him for sending that patient to me and let him know that I'd love to help him with more of his patients. I even offered to come to his office and present information to his team on what Chinese medicine could do to help their patients. He took me up on my offer, and I came to their office several times during lunch and presented on a variety of topics related to the use of Chinese medicine for their types of patients. Consequently, he and other PTs from his office referred a significant number of patients to me.

That entire working relationship was not only great for my practice, in that it brought me heaps of referrals, it was also great for my soul and job satisfaction. I had so much fun working with that particular PT and his entire physical therapy office through the years that followed. I learned a great deal about physical therapy, and hopefully, they learned a lot about Chinese medicine. Besides, we shared a lot of good laughs about the ups and downs in the practice of healthcare. As practitioners, we may have had different modality-specific trainings and education, but we also had a lot in common. Maintaining a simple system like the process described above can benefit everyone. It can lead to:

- More patients
- Educating fellow healthcare professionals about our specific modalities
- Comprehensive healthcare for our patients
- Increased referral pool
- Greater job satisfaction

A circle has no end. It is continuous. *The Golden Circle* offered to you here is similar; it is one in which patients feel valued and thoroughly cared for. They know they can contact you for help with their health, even if you may need to refer them to someone else.

As we leave *The Golden Circle,* here are some takeaways:

PATIENT SATISFACTION SECRETS FROM THE GOLDEN CIRCLE

- Give warm and genuine invitations to treatments.

- Offer easy and immediate scheduling with reminders.

- Ensure that everyone on staff is caring, compassionate, and pleasant.

- Be timely on both ends.

- Agree upon clearly defined expectations.

- Involve family members, caretakers, and/or loved ones.

- Follow up throughout the treatment cycle to monitor compliance and provide support.

- Follow up post-treatment.

- Engage in patient care comanagement.

- Begin (and maintain) a Thank-You-for-Your-Referral system.

CHAPTER 4

Second Stop:
The Healing Temple

The *Healing Temple* reveals important physical factors to consider as part of the overall treatment experience—everything from ease of parking to the comfort of your treatment equipment and space.

LOCATION

Location, location, location. Is your office easy to find with plenty of parking, or are your patients stressed out just getting to your office? I promise you that if this is the case, they will not come back, no matter how great the treatment. How many of you have driven right past your favorite take-out, Starbucks, or another establishment because the line was too long? Choose a location that is easy to find, in a safe part of town, with adequate parking.

Dr. Leena moved her thriving practice to a new office downtown in the belief that her patients would follow her. To her surprise, she was now struggling to bring patients in the door. Why?

As she surveyed the area surrounding her office, she realized that parking was expensive and scarce. Was this the issue? Seeing a parking lot adjacent to her office building, she called the parking lot management company and asked if she could purchase parking passes in bulk quantities. They agreed to sell her one-hour parking passes for $1 each. She then gave these passes out to her patients and advertised the same in her newsletter. Within a few weeks, her practice was rapidly filling up again. She not only got all of her prior patients to come to her new office, she even attracted an additional 30 percent more patients, as other physicians were not offering a parking pass, and this appealed to her patients greatly. This simple $1-per-patient investment paid Dr. Leena back handsomely.

> *Be mindful of adjacent tenants or where you have your practice. I once had my treatment space within a fitness facility where I also taught exercise classes and offered personal training. I thought this would be ideal, because many of my patients were members there. Boy, was I wrong. My treatment room was a little too close to the racquetball courts. Even though my space was extremely tranquil from soundproof padding, the minute my patients left my treatment room, they were bombarded by the sound of racquets and balls. There went all my good work and the patient's relaxation.*

ZENIFY YOUR TREATMENT SPACE

Are your reception, waiting areas, and treatment spaces clean and clear of clutter? A messy treatment space can cause you, and your patients, to feel stressed and anxious.[10] Make sure to get rid of everything that doesn't either have a purpose or bring joy to you and your patients.

This goes for break rooms and your office space as well. These areas need to be clean and organized, or they can consciously or subconsciously create stress for you and your staff.

Practice *feng shui* and the art of Zen in your entire treatment space. Less is more. Every time I move my practice or home, I hire a *feng shui* consultant, and it is worth every penny. People often comment on how warm and comfortable my environments feel to them. Besides, I, too, feel better working and living in these environments. If you cannot find a consultant to help you, I highly recommend at a minimum applying *feng shui* principles to your office space. You can find videos about these principles on YouTube or articles through an internet search. Trust me, you and your patients will benefit greatly from doing so.

Part of the practice of *feng shui* is to clean the energy of your space, as well. This can be accomplished via a variety of methods. Many

---

[10] Carter, Sherrie Bourg. "Why Mess Causes Stress: 8 Reasons, 8 Remedies." Psychology Today. Sussex Publishers. Accessed June 21, 2019. https://www.psychologytoday.com/us/blog/high-octane-women/201203/why-mess-causes-stress-8-reasons-8-remedies.

people use a method called "smudging," which is an ancient technique of burning dried sage leaves. It has been believed for centuries across a number of cultures, including the Native American people, that doing so removes negative spirits and energies. On a more scientific level, it has been actually proven that this process kills 94 percent of germs and bacteria in the air.[11]

Killing negative energy and germs? Seeing that many patients bring at least one of those things to our spaces, this seems like a good practice.

Other ways to clear and cleanse the energy in your space include:

Frequently open all window and doors. This allows fresh air to move through the space while also allowing direct sunlight to bathe the rooms.

Burn *palo santo*, aka "saints wood," in your space. Use it as you would the dried sage leaves. I like to call *palo santo* "Heaven's campfire" because of how it smells. An added bonus is that it has been used in parts of the world like Ecuador and Peru to repel mosquitos and other insects.

---

[11] Nautiyal, Chandra Shekhar, Puneet Singh Chauhan, and Yeshwant Laxman Nene. "Medicinal Smoke Reduces Airborne Bacteria." *Journal of Ethnopharmacology* 114, no. 3 (2007): 446–51. https://doi.org/10.1016/j.jep.2007.08.038.

Use sandalwood incense. This has been used by many cultures in rituals with the intention of driving out negativity and transforming the space to one of positivity.

Use air purifiers. These can also help to circulate and cleanse the air in your treatment spaces.

At our first stop, *The Golden Circle*, I talked about how the Chopra Center employs a team approach to providing healthcare to their guests. They also set the bar in terms of establishing ambiance and a Zen-like healing temple.

Gorgeous environments, tranquil spaces, nurturing foods, gentle yoga instruction, herbal supplementation, meditation rooms, ancient and unique healing massage therapy sessions, one-on-one appointments with a western medical doctor (MD) and other healthcare practitioners are just some of the offerings each guest receives. They leave no detail overlooked. The center's staff ensure that all guests who participate in their retreats, events, and/or services are made to feel genuinely loved, cared for, and in competent hands. On top of all this, they treat their staff the same way, with the same love, gentleness, compassion, and royalty-like status.

These may seem like subtle elements to the treatment experience, but when they are problematic, they can prevent you from creating the relaxing, rejuvenating, healing space you desire.

Be Your Own Patient

Lie on your treatment tables from time to time to make sure they are still comfortable. Test your heat lamps. Use your equipment on yourself. Try on your eye pillows. Sample the products you sell. Stare up at your treatment room ceilings. Look at all the walls and down at the floor. Are they clean, soothing, and comfortable?

A few years ago, I noticed one of my headrests looked worn, so I went shopping on Amazon. I found a reasonably priced headrest with 1,300 reviews that averaged 4.5 stars. Perfect, right? So, I bought two and installed them immediately upon arrival.

About two weeks into using these new headrests, I entered a treatment room. My patient had removed his head from the headrest. He was lying with his head turned sideways, cheek to table. This would have been fine had he not had needles in his neck and back. *Yikes.*

After removing all the needles as fast as I could, I asked him why he moved. He told me that the headrest was so unbearably uncomfortable that he just couldn't take it any longer. I apologized profusely. When he left, I placed my own face into the face cradle. *Ouch!* Instant headache. That poor guy was there for twenty minutes. Even worse, I had about ten other patients who used those headrests before and likely had the same horrible experience.

Moral of the story: *Preview your equipment.* Try it before your patients do.

Music Is Medicine

In several pockets of the United States, ambulances are now playing music in the back with the patients. It was found that certain music during transport improved the patient outcomes. Likewise, hospitals offer music in patient rooms and operating rooms for the same reason. Music can heal, and science is now proving it.[12]

Do you provide music? If so, do you change it frequently? I once stopped going to a therapist that I had been seeing weekly for several months because she played the same exact music every week. She was terrific and highly skilled at her therapy. In fact, she was the only specialist in that technique for 100 miles, but there came a point in time for me at which that music was no longer soothing and started to negate any benefits I was receiving in the session.

[12] Myers, Katie L. Florida State University Thesis: "The Use of Patient-Preferred Music to Improve Patient Experience during Interfacility Ambulance Transport." September, 2013. https://fsu.digital.flvc.org/islandora/object/fsu:185145/datastream/PDF/view

Moral of the story: *Change your music.*

Taken a step further, ask your patients what type of music soothes them. Maybe your patient doesn't want any music at all during treatment. I was enlightened to this idea while leading a class on interprofessional communication in the doctoral program for Chinese medicine. We were discussing music during a treatment session, and a student reported that one of his patients got angry because the assistant left him in a room with music playing when he *really* just wanted peace and quiet.

Are you in an office where providing music is a challenge, or there is intrusive noise from adjacent rooms? Something I have found to be incredibly useful in these situations is to get personal earbud-style headphones for each patient. As a courtesy, store these in a small box with the patient's name on it for when they return for their next session. You can buy headphones in bulk quantity for a very reasonable price, and your patients can enjoy soothing music at their desired volume level regardless of disruptive neighbors or environments.

AROMATHERAPY

It has been clinically proven that when aromatherapy is added to massage, acupuncture treatment, or acupressure treatments, outcomes are more significant than providing any of those modalities alone.[13] In fact, while obtaining my doctorate degree, I conducted a clinical trial wherein I proved that when aromatherapy was added to an acupuncture treatment aimed at reducing stress, it was more effective than acupuncture alone.[14]

You can provide aromatherapy to your patients in a variety of ways. Some include the use of essential oils, and some are even more simple. Just as when presenting music to your patients, it behooves you to *ask* if they want aromatherapy before deciding to provide it to them. They may have sensitivities or aversions to certain oils and/or smells.

Essential Oil Diffusers. First, you can use essential oils in diffusers. If you choose this method, here are a few caveats. (1) Make sure the diffuser has an automatic shutoff feature. You don't want to be home wondering if you left the diffuser on. (2) Less is more. Start with subtle levels. After a while, you will become inured to the scent and maybe not even notice it. You may be tempted to turn up the dial on the diffuser—don't do it. Too much aromatherapy can repel patients and border on being harmful. Also, think about this: Using a diffuser is a one-for-all approach. It can become quite a challenge to find aromatherapy

[13] Shin, Byung-Cheul, and Myeong Soo Lee. "Effects of Aromatherapy Acupressure on Hemiplegic Shoulder Pain And Motor Power in Stroke Patients: A Pilot Study." *The Journal of Alternative and Complementary Medicine* 13, no. 2 (2007): 247–52. https://doi.org/10.1089/acm.2006.6189.

[14] Haradin, East. "Combining Acupuncture with Aromatherapy to Enhance the Treatment of Stress." Meridians Journal of Acupuncture and Oriental Medicine, 2018. https://www.meridiansjaom.com/vol-6-no-2-abstracts.html.

that appeals to everyone. Therefore, I like to use the following methods, which offer personalized aromatherapy.

Personalized Aromatherapy. Drop essential oils onto a cotton ball; place it on the patient's chest or within their sniff zone. The patient can then enjoy the aromatic benefits from the saturated cotton ball while getting treated. I've also used *White Flower,* an inexpensive Chinese herbal liniment, as aromatherapy on a cotton ball. Patients love it, and the beneficial effect of the spearmint oil in *White Flower* reduces pain.

You can also make your own aromatherapy sprays with different essential oils for specific conditions. For example, you can make a spray for calming and soothing a patient, or one for pain relief.

Recipes and instructions for making personalized aromatherapy sprays are provided in Appendix E.

Rose water. In my opinion, simple rose water is a perfect gateway into aromatherapy. It is super mild, affordable, and can easily be found in any natural food store. Spray rose water in your office, on your patients, on your treatment table, and/or on your eye pillows. You can even spray rose water onto a tissue and lay the other side of the tissue across the eyes of your patient instead of an eye pillow.

Simple and natural aromatherapy. Fresh flowers that have a pleasant smell, like tuberose, carnations, gardenias, or roses, are a form of aromatherapy. In addition, fragrant plants are also effective. Place some fresh lavender or rosemary in a vase with water and let these subtle, plant-sourced aromatherapy methods provide your patients with a sense of calm, relaxation, cleanliness, and clarity.

Prepare Your Hands Beyond Sanitizer

What do your hands smell like? As healthcare practitioners, we frequently use our hands for adjustments, palpation, treatments, you name it. It's assumed that you are frequently washing your hands, but have you ever wondered, or even cared about, how your hands smell? Do your hands smell like the onions and garlic you had for lunch or like hand sanitizer?

Here's a wonderful and easy two-for-one. Spray your hands with an aromatherapy spray. That way, your hands get a cleansing boost from the anti-microbial nature of essential oils, and you provide aromatherapy to your patients via your hands.

(Again, while the spray-your-hands method is easy and effective, I recommend that you first ask your patients if they would like to receive aromatherapy in the first place. They may want a scent-free experience.)

Gemstones

I'm a rock hound and always have been. This means I have a love for crystals, gemstones, and rocks. I have them tastefully displayed in my office, and they seem to act like a little army of warriors vibrating out healing energy for my patients. My patients often comment on them and remark that they feel comforted by their presence. I've even had patients hold onto gemstones in their palms during treatments—a golf-ball-sized rose quartz to heal a hurting heart; a polished chunk of labradorite ("The Angel Stone") to help hear guidance from guardian angels; blue calcite to reduce pain, soothe arthritis, or help a patient speak their truth; some amethyst to bring bodies back into balance. While healing from gemstones has not yet been scientifically proven, it was determined from a study consisting of 400 participants that more than half were aware of gemstone therapy, and 39 percent believed that gemstones have an impact on health.[15]

Meditation

Meditation has been proven to grow back grey matter in the brain while improving the energy of a space.[16] Therefore, meditating in your treatment space is a sacred two-for-one.

---

[15] Sidra Ishaque, Taimur Saleem, and Waris Qidwai. "Knowledge, Attitudes and Practices Regarding Gemstone Therapeutics in a Selected Adult Population in Pakistan." *BMC Complementary and Alternative Medicine.* BioMed Central, August 26, 2009. https://doi.org/10.1186/1472-6882-9-32.

[16] Last, Nicole, Emily Tufts, and Leslie E Auger. "The Effects of Meditation on Grey Matter Atrophy and Neurodegeneration: A Systematic Review." *Journal of Alzheimer's Disease: JAD.* US National Library of Medicine, 2017. https://www.ncbi.nlm.nih.gov/pubmed/27983555.

Between patients, I meditate in my treatment room—even if it is just for a few minutes. Without fail, after I have meditated in my treatment space, patients have asked me questions like, "Did you do something different to the room? Did you get new furniture? Did you have the room painted?" No. I just meditated in it. Meditating in your space costs you nothing, and the reward is an improvement to both the energy of your treatment space and your mind.

While I could go on and on about the benefits of aromatherapy, gemstones, meditation and the like, we have more stops on this road trip. It's time to go.

Here are your takeaways from *The Healing Temple*:

Patient Satisfaction Secrets From The Healing Temple

- Set your practice in a good location.

- Provide adequate parking.

- Create a warm ambiance.

- Clear your space of clutter.

- Practice the art of *feng shui*.

- Be your own patient.

- Incorporate music into your sessions.

- Offer personal headphones to shield distracting sounds.

- Include aromatherapy with your sessions.

- Prepare your hands.

- Add gemstones to the environment.

- Meditate in your space.

CHAPTER 5

Third Stop: The Great Sage

The *Great Sage* represents you—moreover, the greatest and best version of yourself. In order for you to provide exceptional experiences, you need to be completely present and in alignment. During our stop here and visit with *The Great Sage,* we will explore ways in which you can achieve this.

YOU ARE A VESSEL

Imagine you are very thirsty and I offer you some water in a dirty paper cup. If you are thirsty enough, you may drink it. But wouldn't you rather have that water in a beautifully handcrafted, sparkling-clean crystal glass? The answer is obvious, and in this metaphor, you are the cup. You are a conduit for healing, a vessel of sorts. Do you deliver health care and healing from a dirty paper cup or a pristine crystal glass?

We all know what we need to do to be the best versions of ourselves: eat healthy and nurturing foods, get adequate sleep, continue our studies, move and/or exercise daily, meditate, practice moderation and mindfulness, and maintain a healthy work-life balance. Are you doing those things, or are you robotically treating patients when you really don't want to be treating them or cannot be present for them?

What are you doing to continuously grow, improve, and be the best practitioner you can be? Do you "walk your talk"? Are you an excellent example for your patients? Are you aligned with your passions, or do you honestly dislike what you are doing, like the day spa massage practitioner I told you about in chapter 1? Are you burned out?

GET INTO ALIGNMENT

If you don't like treating people, or if patient care does not bring you genuine joy and fulfillment, please find another way to contribute to medicine and healthcare. I assure you, there are endless ways in which you can stay in your chosen field. Would you want to be treated by someone who didn't really want to treat patients? You may think you are faking it, but people can tell.

Continuing to practice in healthcare when you don't want to is unfair to everyone. First, it is unfair to your patients, who deserve care from someone who really wants to treat them. Second, it is unfair to yourself; you deserve to be totally thrilled and fulfilled by your profession. Finally, it is unfair to the passionate practitioner in your field who wants to treat patients; you are preventing that by holding onto patients you don't even want.

WALK YOUR TALK. BE A ROLE MODEL

While I was on my journey to find my life's purpose and passion, I attended hypnotherapy school. The school was owned and run by a husband-and-wife team who had been practicing and teaching hypnotherapy for many years. I was fascinated by the mind's abilities and dove deep into my studies. The information was incredible, and I loved studying something so different from my undergraduate business degree.

But I did not complete the program.

One afternoon, I drove home after successfully passing my six-month competency exams and completing all required courses for level 1 hypnotherapy. Something behind the school building caught my eye. It was someone smoking. In fact, it was one of the owners and teachers of the hypnotherapy school. I couldn't erase that visual from my mind for the entire forty-five minutes it took me to drive home. By the time I reached my house, I had decided that I wasn't going to continue the program. That single event ruined it for me. If the owners and teachers couldn't stop smoking (which hypnotherapy is known to support), how was I going to believe in this healing method or its ability to help others?

A saying that has been around for ages is "Nobody likes a skinny chef." I'm not suggesting we all go out and get fat. Instead, I am proposing that we show up for the very same lectures we are giving our patients. I encourage you to try a protocol for yourself so you can speak from experience. Holding yourself to higher standards gives your patients motivation to do the same.

BE A LIGHTHOUSE

In a sense, you are a lighthouse for your patients and potential patients. People are seeking your specific talents, insight, guidance, information, and/or healing style. Be clear on what you want to offer and how you want to provide it so that you attract the boats you want to come to your harbor.

For example, let's say you love treating women's health issues but don't necessarily enjoy treating pediatric patients. To attract your perfect patients, you should become known as the thought leader in women's health and place yourself in situations and settings where those types of patients would be found. Refer pediatric patients to a friend or colleague who loves to treat that demographic.

If you hate working on the weekends, do not hold office hours on the weekend, no matter what. Not even if you find a really inexpensive treatment space on the weekends in the best part of town. You will subconsciously sabotage your own success because deep down, you don't want to work on the weekends. You will find excuses not to go into your office on the weekends, or you will dread going into the office when you do. That is projecting the wrong type of energy into your practice. It will repel patients, I promise. I've seen it in so many practitioners over the years. We used to call it "willing our patients away."

Let's say you love bringing your dog to work, but some patients don't like having Milo at the office. Letting your lighthouse shine bright would mean you would politely let patients know that you bring your dog Milo to the office and he will be available for additional pet therapy at no charge. The patients you lose by welcoming your dog to the office will open space for the patients who receive additional healing energy from having the dog present. And the biggest bonus lies within you—no guilt for leaving Milo home, and a feeling of full career satisfaction because you have your best friend with you all day.

When you genuinely want to treat patients, your raging desire will draw patients to you. It will be evident when you tell people what you do for a living. Your friends and family will want to send people to you. The clearer you are on where you want to treat, how you want to treat, when you want to treat, and whom you want to treat, the brighter your light. The brighter the light in your lighthouse, the more boats you will attract from near and far.

I once learned another rather nontraditional way of encouraging prior patients to return for treatments. At one of my favorite wellness centers where I worked, one of the other physicians and I would periodically practice this ritual, and each and every time, it resulted in patients calling within the following week to book appointments with us.

We would go through our patient files, open them up, and send love and good feelings directly to our patients through their charts. With each chart open, we would reflect upon our patients and connect with the good feelings we had while working with them. I cannot explain why it worked, exactly; I can just tell you that it did work for us, and it works for many other people with whom I have shared this technique who have tried it for themselves. You might want to try it. At a minimum, it's a lovely feel-good exercise in gratitude, reflecting on the lives that you have touched and that have touched your heart.

Healer Heal Thyself, Healer Know Thyself

In the spring of 2013, I had a thriving practice, and life was going full speed ahead. I had just moved to Orange County from San Diego and was finally gaining positive momentum in my practice, getting acclimated to the Orange County culture.

I'll never forget the phone call I received on one Tuesday afternoon. A very unexpected phone call. My father called to tell me that my mother had stopped breathing and that they were taking her to the hospital. "OK," I thought, "Dad will get there, and she'll be OK, and I'll go visit her tomorrow while she recovers from whatever made her stop breathing."

Then I got another phone call. This one was from my brother.

"Mom's dead."

What? This didn't make any sense. Dad said she wasn't breathing, and they were taking her to the hospital, I thought to myself.

"East. Dad doesn't know how to tell you. She is gone," were the last words I heard my brother say before I dropped the phone in shock and disbelief.

They buried my mother that Friday. I went into work the following Tuesday because I had a full load of patients scheduled. Yes, it was one week after my mother had unexpectedly passed away, but I didn't want to let anyone down.

By the end of the day treating patients, I could barely stand erect. It was all I could do to not weep with every patient. My mind was not in the treatment rooms or focused on any of my patients. I was an empty shell giving treatments like a robot.

As I drove home that night, I knew I couldn't hold a space for my patients. I could barely maintain a healing space for myself. I made the decision right then to take time off from my private practice until I felt 100 percent ready to come back and be completely present for others. That took six months. I grieved, I healed, and when I started to feel I might be ready to treat patients, I waited until the desire to treat patients was bursting out of me, almost as if I couldn't contain it anymore. Only then was I ready to return. Had I returned any earlier, it would have been too soon.

I recognize that this is an extreme example, but it begs the question: Do you need to retreat and recharge? Are you able to hold a healing space for your patients, or do you need to seek healing for yourself?

WATCH YOUR LANGUAGE

Speaking of mothers: They often tell us to watch our language, don't they? I'm going to suggest the same thing, but from a different perspective.

Let's say a patient comes to you with left knee pain, infertility, or insomnia. Do you say things like, "I'm going to treat your bad knee" or "I see from your chart that you are infertile" or "I see you are an insomniac"?

Our patients come to us with a diagnosis of a condition, or signs and symptoms of a condition they are currently experiencing.

These things do not define our patients. Your patient has an affected knee and an unaffected knee, not a bad knee and a good knee. You have a patient who is experiencing challenges becoming pregnant. You have a patient who is having trouble staying asleep or falling asleep.

What if we started to replace words like *bad* and *good* with *affected* or *unaffected*? We could tell our patients that they are experiencing certain signs and/or symptoms rather than labeling them.

Better yet, what if we saw our patients as completely whole, perfectly healthy and well? If we don't do this, who will? So often, other practitioners and even the loved ones of our patients have given up hope for recovery. It's even worse when our patients give up hope on themselves. They need at least one person to believe in them, and in the possibility of recovery, relief, healing, and/or miracles.

Are your words encouraging? Do you speak with words that are positive and offer hope, or are you clinical, monotonous, using language (verbal or even nonverbal) that can contribute to a nocebo effect? Studies have shown that the language and behavior of the practitioner can have a placebo or nocebo effect on the patient similar to that of drugs.[17] Are your choices of words

[17] Daniali, Hojjat, and Magne Arve Flaten. "A Qualitative Systematic Review of Effects of Provider Characteristics and Nonverbal Behavior on Pain, and Placebo and Nocebo Effects." *Frontiers in Psychiatry*, Frontiers Media S.A., 15 Apr. 2019, www.ncbi.nlm.nih.gov/pubmed/31037059.

contributing to placebo, Latin for "to please," or nocebo, which loosely translates to the mean "I will harm"?

I've had two children, and during both pregnancies, I had to go in twice a week for what is referred to as a nonstress test (NST). If you are not familiar with these tests, they are boring. A nurse places two straps over your enlarged belly to measure the movements and heartbeat of the baby. With my first pregnancy, the nurses were pretty average and typical. Not much was discussed when I came in. The nurse strapped me in for twenty minutes, looked over the printout from the machine, and would say, "OK, you can go."

I didn't even think about the experience until I had my second child and a different nurse gave me the NST. She always used positive and encouraging words, saying things like, "Baby looks beautiful," or, "Everything is perfect." She could have used plain language, like, "Your tests are normal, you can go." Instead, this delightful woman used warm, encouraging language that made me feel safe and cared for, which helped a great deal since I was an older mom (over thirty-five years old), assigned the label "geriatric pregnancy."

It is easy to be unconscious and unintentional in our speech. I want to encourage you to practice more mindfulness in this regard. Be intentional with your word choices and deliberate in the words you choose rather than letting just anything escape your mouth while your thoughts are somewhere else. I once was in a training session, and the presenter was providing us with really good information. She ended what she said with this sentence: "So, keep that in the back of your little minds and make sure you remember it." Well, I never forgot that she called my mind little, that's for sure. And I cannot tell you anything else she may have shared with us that day. After she said that (probably completely unintentionally) she lost all respect and credibility from me. From the looks on the faces of others in that training session, I'm sure she lost a few more with that flippant comment, as well.

MEDITATION

Meditation is also helpful, even if it is only three minutes between patients, as mentioned previously in chapter 4 (*The Healing Temple*). I have made it a habit to come to work early and meditate before my day begins, and I often meditate between patients. If I'm crunched for time, I select a three-minute long song and play it, meditating for only as long as that song. Even that small amount of time makes a huge difference. Some songs, like "Weightless" by Marconi Union, have even been clinically proven to reduce anxiety up to 65 percent.[18]

I get it—life can be tough at times, and we are human beings, after all. We get overly stressed, experience loss, go through heartbreaks,

---

[18] "Neuroscientists Discover A Song That Reduces Anxiety By 65 Percent (Listen)." Collective Evolution, May 22, 2018. https://www.collective-evolution.com/2016/12/25/neuroscientists-discover-a-song-that-reduces-anxiety-by-65-percent-listen/.

health issues, financial difficulties, and the like. These challenging times can easily bring us down. I propose to you that this is when we need whatever it takes to raise our energy levels. We owe it to our patients. We owe it to ourselves. It is imperative that you practice proper self-care. You absolutely must engage in activities that feed your soul. Just as on an airplane, you need to place the oxygen mask on yourself first. If you don't take care of yourself, your body and soul will seek your attention by giving you more things to slow you down and make you stop. Prevention is the best medicine. Practicing proper self-care ensures that you never break down.

Only *you* know what really does it for you. Therefore, it's up to you to participate in those activities when you find yourself not feeling as good as you could. You will find a method in appendix C that will help you to quickly and effectively raise your vibration, anytime and anywhere.

Be true to yourself. You are healing your patients, but you are also influencing them with your attitude and energy. Make sure that you infect them with passion, with hope, with enthusiasm, and with a genuine love for life.

To that end, here are some takeaways from our time with *The Great Sage*:

PATIENT SATISFACTION SECRETS FROM THE GREAT SAGE

- Be a clean vessel.

- Be in alignment with yourself.

- Be a positive role model.

- Let your lighthouse shine bright.

- Heal thyself when needed.

- Watch your language.

- Meditate, even if for a moment.

- Practice self-care to prevent burnout.

- Keep your energy, mood, and vibration high.

CHAPTER 6

Last Stop: The Giving Forest

The *Giving Forest* can be as thick or sparse as you want it to be. It can be as clinical or mystical as you would like to make it. *The Giving Forest* offers the patient little gifts that may cost you next to nothing, but which create immeasurable value. Some of the offerings are tangible giveaways, and some are intangible; kind gestures that go beyond your call of duty, or adjunctive modalities that add value to the overall experiences we provide.

INTANGIBLE GIFTS

I once had the privilege of treating an incredibly sweet, gentle-natured thirty-two-year-old elementary school teacher. For the sake of this story, let's call her Erica.

Erica and her husband had been trying to conceive for nearly three years with no success. She was frustrated and came to Chinese medicine as a last resort before trying western medical interventions (intrauterine insemination, in vitro fertilization, and the like).

Erica reported that both she and her husband had been checked for medical reasons causing infertility and that the tests had come back inconclusive. Her primary care doctor told her to be patient and that it would happen when it was meant to happen. This answer wasn't reassuring to her. She wanted to get pregnant now.

After three months of weekly acupuncture sessions with me and taking Chinese herbs, she woke on day twenty-nine of her menstrual cycle to yet another period. She wasn't pregnant—again. She came to see me that day feeling very depressed and defeated.

"I have an idea," I said to Erica. "It's a little out there, but if you are game, let's ask the angels for some guidance," I offered, as I pulled out a box of Doreen Virtue Angel Oracle Cards.

"Oh, I don't know," said Erica. "Are those like tarot cards?"

"No, not at all," I replied. "They are all positive and are believed to give us messages from our guardian angels and the Divine."

"Let's not do it. I'm scared," she said.

"I understand, Erica. It's been a tough road for you. Maybe the cards can help you understand why it is taking so long," I offered.

"Well, OK. What do I do?" she asked.

"Shuffle the cards and pull one out from the deck. It can come from the top, the middle, anywhere. Pull any card you want," I instructed.

Erica shuffled the deck and pulled a card from the middle of the deck. She turned it over and as we looked at the card our mouths nearly dropped to the floor. The card was titled "Child." It had a picture of a mother holding a baby.

Erica started to cry.

Then she looked up at me with a skeptical, almost questioning look and said, "Wait a second. Are they all *Child* cards?" She said.

I turned over the remaining forty-four cards to prove to her that no, they were not all *Child* cards.

That's when one more card fell from the deck and landed face down onto the floor between us.

I reached down, picked up the fallen card, and turned it over so we could see what the card said. It was the card titled *Have Confidence.*

Erica and I laughed, and as she wiped more tears from her eyes, my eyes joined in on the waterworks going on.

Erica did not get her period the following month. She got pregnant and gave birth to one of the most beautiful babies I have ever seen.

That is a story of an intangible type of thing we can incorporate into our sessions to add value. This is an example of something that is out of the norm, out of the ordinary, or at least offers a sense of magic and hope to patients who have faced challenges in their healing journey.

> *There are tiny cards called* Angel Cards *that have positive sayings on them. You can place these at the reception desk or have patients pull one before they leave. Small little gifts are unique and add massive value to the experience.*

HOLDING A SPACE FOR YOUR PATIENTS

I am sometimes asked, "What does it mean to hold a space for someone?" It means you have compassion for where that person is in their life journey, without judgment. You see that person whole, healed, and perfect, no matter what they may be presenting to you. So often, much of the medical community (possibly even the patient's own support system) has given up. What if you are their only hope for finding their way back to wellness? What if you are the only person who believes in the patient when the patient doesn't even believe in him- or herself? Do you think Lance Armstrong stayed with the physicians who told him he would never cycle again, or did he find physicians who were determined to bring him back to health?

I used to trade treatments with a colleague of mine. Each month, we would give one another treatments—on different days—and they typically lasted about forty-five minutes.

On one of the days when it was my turn to receive a treatment, I arrived at his office in quite a frazzled and enraged state. Something had me extremely upset, and we spent about forty minutes, just talking. I finally said to him, "OK, well, I feel better. When do you want to start my treatment?"

"You just received it," he replied.

At first, I was taken aback. I had come for an acupuncture treatment. But you know what? He was right. Honestly, I cannot even remember what had gotten me so upset. However, I *do* remember that just talking with him and having him genuinely listen to me, holding a space for me, made me feel 100 percent better. Being totally present for your patients is a gift in and of itself.

Simply expressing genuine compassion end empathy for a patient has been proven to increase clinical outcomes. This is a good place to start, and as you feel more comfortable with holding a deeper and wider space for your patients, you will see it happen almost organically. Then you will be able to answer this question for yourself.[19]

SITTING WITH YOUR PATIENTS

Just sitting down with patients while you converse will give them the impression you have spent more time with them. This has even been proven. A study was conducted: a doctor either stood at the door, walked in the room, or sat with patients while discussing their cases. In all three conditions, the doctor spent the exact same amount of time with patients. However, the patients in the rooms where the doctor sat down reported a greater perception of elapsed time than those with the doctor standing at the door or in the room, even when it was five minutes.[20]

I first learned of this phenomenon in perception from listing to Victoria Sweet speak on what she refers to as "slow medicine." In her TED talk, lectures, and books, *Slow Medicine* and *God's Hotel*, Victoria, a seasoned and experienced western MD, shares

[19] Hojat, Mohammadreza, Daniel Z Louis, Fred W Markham, Richard Wender, Carol Rabinowitz, and Joseph S Gonnella. "Physicians' Empathy and Clinical Outcomes for Diabetic Patients." *Academic Medicine: Journal of the Association of American Medical Colleges*. U.S. National Library of Medicine, March 2011. https://www.ncbi.nlm.nih.gov/pubmed/21248604

[20] Swayden, Kelli J, Karen K Anderson, Lynne M Connelly, Jennifer S Moran, Joan K McMahon, and Paul M Arnold. "Effect of Sitting vs. Standing on Perception of Provider Time at Bedside: a Pilot Study." *Patient Education and Counseling*. U.S. National Library of Medicine, February 2012. https://www.ncbi.nlm.nih.gov/pubmed/21719234.

her insights into the almost magical healing benefits of simply providing basic comforts to patients. Her work to deliver these messages is breaking the ice of cold, clinical-style patient care and reminding physicians all over the world of the healing power of genuine compassion and empathy.

In Chinese medicine, we take a person's pulse as part of the diagnosis. The twelve major organ systems are represented in the pulses, so when we are taking the pulse, we may hold the pulse for a few minutes. The pulses we examine are below the patient's wrists—six on the right side and six on the left.

When I take a patient's pulse, I like to do it with the patient lying face-up on the treatment table, and I sit next to the patient on the table, holding both wrists at the same time. I feel this is a more personal approach and creates good rapport with the patient and a genuine connection. Alex Tiberi did this during treatments. He was a fantastic role model for the comforting bedside manner and human connection.

ANOINTING YOUR PATIENT'S FEET

What the heck is anointing feet? Isn't that something mentioned in the Bible?

Yes.

The healing practice of anointing feet goes back that far. What is it? In simple terms, it is giving someone a foot massage.

Before a patient gets ready to leave, I might ask, "May I anoint your feet?" As you might suspect, at first people almost always give me a puzzled look and say something like, "Uh, OK," or "I guess so," or even, "What's that?"

To these comments, I reply with something like, "All you have to do is relax and receive this ancient method of honoring your body's ability to heal itself. The soles of your feet are little maps of your entire body, and by massaging them, I am, in essence, harmonizing your entire body." In anointing their feet, I might gently press on some of the acupressure points located there, but I am mainly just giving the energy and intention of love, healing, and nurturing to my patients. In my mind, I might even say a little prayer to the Divine/Universe/God: "Please bring this person the exact energy and/or people they need to be complete, whole, and healed."

Adjunctive Modalities

Clinical evidence is now beginning to prove the efficacy of several widely used adjunctive modalities within alternative medicine: specifically, modalities such as Reiki and Healing Touch. In one study, researchers found that Reiki reduced heart rate and diastolic blood pressure more significantly than the non-Reiki control groups.[21] Another study confirmed Reiki's effect on heart rate and found that real Reiki vs sham Reiki had a way of bringing heart rate into homeostasis.[22] The efficacy of Healing Touch was demonstrated in a separate trial where it was found to significantly reduce pain and stress levels.[23]

Another adjunctive modality worth mentioning is the incorporation of oracle or angel cards, as described in the story above about the fertility patient. You can find a variety of styles and themes in oracle or angel cards; perhaps one matches up with your practice.

Again, these are subtle, intangible additions to a treatment session that may just be what sets you apart from the norm and provides your patient with the message and/or breakthrough he or she needs.

TANGIBLE GIVEAWAYS

We can also give physical gifts to our patients. The following small, extremely affordable gifts from us during our treatment sessions

---

[21] Mackay, Nicola, Stig Hansen, and Oona McFarlane. "Autonomic Nervous System Changes during Reiki Treatment: a Preliminary Study." *The Journal of Alternative and Complementary Medicine* (New York, N.Y.). U.S. National Library of Medicine, December 2004. https://www.ncbi.nlm.nih.gov/pubmed/15674004/.

[22] Baldwin, Ann Linda, Christina Wagers, and Gary E Schwartz. "Reiki Improves Heart Rate Homeostasis in Laboratory Rats." *The Journal of Alternative and Complementary Medicine* (New York, N.Y.). U.S. National Library of Medicine, May 2008. https://www.ncbi.nlm.nih.gov/pubmed/18435597.

[23] Wilkinson, Dawn S., Pamela L. Chatman, James E. Johnson, Terrance L. Barbour, Nilufer Barbour, Yvonne Myles, and Antonio Reel. "The Clinical Effectiveness of Healing Touch." *The Journal of Alternative and Complementary Medicine*, Vol. 8, No. 1, 2004. https://www.liebertpub.com/doi/abs/10.1089/107555302753507168.

can go a long way in terms of increasing patient satisfaction, retention, patient referrals, and increasing the perceived value of your services. The little investment on our behalf can pay us back handsomely.

Aromatherapy on cotton balls. During treatment sessions, I typically place an aromatherapy-saturated cotton ball on the patient's upper chest near their sternum (or within their "sniff zone" if they are face-down). After the treatment, I give the patient the cotton ball to take home with them. I instruct them to continue to inhale the aromatherapy periodically, which will keep the treatment coursing through their body. It's a very inexpensive gift that patients treasure. I once walked a patient to her car and saw a line of cotton balls on her dashboard. She told me that she keeps all the cotton balls I give her after treatment, and that she just "loves them."

Tea. *Gan Mao Da Zao Tang* (sometimes referred to as "Happy Tea") is a simple yet powerful Chinese herbal formula that contains three herbs (Chinese date/jujube fruit [*Da Zao*], licorice root [*Gan Cao*], and barley seed [*Fu Xia Mai*]) and has been proven to have a strong anti-depressant effect.[24] You can offer this tea in the waiting room for patients to sample. Because

---

[24] Huang, Hsiang-Ling, Swee-Ling Lim, Lu Kuan-Hung, and Lee-Yan Sheen. "Antidepressant-like Effects of Gan-Mai-Dazao-Tang via Monoamine Regulatory Pathways on Forced Swimming Test in Rats." Journal of Traditional and Complementary Medicine. Elsevier, March 3, 2017. https://www.sciencedirect.com/science/article/pii/S2225411017300123.

the ingredients are so simple and easy to acquire, you can also give your patients a small baggie with single-dose amounts of the herbs for them to prepare for themselves at home. Passionflower or kava tea are both excellent for relaxation. You can buy these at any natural foods store or online. Yogi Teas are great quality and have beautiful, wise sayings on the tea bags. You can offer a variety of Yogi teas in your waiting room and let patients sip them while they wait or even take some home with them after they are finished.

Licorice sticks. Dried licorice root sticks (*Gan Cao*) are used in nearly all Chinese medicine herbal formulas. Licorice is harmonizing and helps bring the mind, body, and soul into balance. I always keep a jar of *Gan Cao* sticks in my office. Oftentimes, I will place a few sticks in a cup of hot water and have patients sip the herbal water before or after treatment. *Gan Cao* hot water is especially helpful for the initial onset of the common cold where there is a slight sore throat. Soothing and harmonizing, this inexpensive little giveaway goes a long way in creating a natural and unique healing experience for patients.

HEALTHY FOOD SAMPLE AND SNACKS

Chia seeds are a great source of omega-3s. I give patients small baggies with chia seeds in them and tell them to add the chia seeds to yogurt, salad dressing, smoothies, muffin mixes, etc. It's a great way to get them to try chia seeds and see how they can easily add them to their diets.

Goji berries are a Chinese herb and wonderful source of antioxidants and healing nutrients for the body and eyes. Just like chia seeds, I give patients little bags of goji berries after their treatment session and instruct them to add them to oatmeal, yogurt, tea, muffin mixes, etc. I often add about ten goji berries to a cup of hot water and let the patient take it home with them after their session. To me, it may be a simple and inexpensive Chinese herb, but to my patient, it is an ancient healing berry that they learned about from me.

Omega-3 trail mix packets can be found at Trader Joe's and other natural food stores. I like to have these on hand at my office for my patients in case they are hungry. These little packs of healthy trail mix containing almonds, cranberries, walnuts, and cashews cost pennies but add value to your session.

You can lead a horse to water, but can't necessarily make it drink. But what if the horse hasn't tried water? What if you give that horse its first taste of water and the horse realizes how good it is?

That's the theory behind bringing in healthy food and snacks for my patients. So often in the past, when I had given recipes or healthy food options to my patients, they wouldn't make the recipes for themselves.

"It doesn't look like it would taste good."

"I don't even know where to find the ingredients."

"Yeah, I know. I've been meaning to make some of that." These are some of the comments I would hear from patients when I asked if they had made the recipe or tried a healthier food alternative.

Therefore, in addition to the items listed above, I bring in food samples of the types of foods I encourage my patients to eat, such as quinoa and/or brown rice pasta to replace meals made with gluten, room temperature smoothies to replace frozen ones, seaweed, goji berry oatmeal, and muffins and bread sweetened with orange juice rather than sugar. They are more likely to make these foods for themselves if they have tasted them first.

At-A-Glance Calendars

I remember a day when everyone used at-a-glance calendars. It was great to be able to see the whole month at once. Now, most people use their cell phones for scheduling. This doesn't mean we should get rid of the old at-a-glance calendars. I have found them to be extremely helpful. I purchase a big lot of them every year for $1 each and give them to patients.

You can find at-a-glance calendars with images such as puppies, kittens, kites, rainbows, or inspirational sayings on the cover and hand them out according to the personalities of your patients. Patients can use these purse-sized calendars to record their treatment progress. They can record episodes and/or occurrences of specific symptoms. They can write down medications taken, foods eaten, lifestyle situations that may be contributing to their condition. You can ask them to bring in their calendars each week and review their progress together. It's a $1 gift from you that creates a more objective measurement of your treatment plan efficacy while benefiting the overall experience for the patient. It has been my experience that this method also increases patient compliance while it brings additional awareness to patients.

PRODUCT SAMPLES

Be generous with samples of products you sell in your clinic. You can open a bottle of supplements and give patients small samples to try before they commit to purchasing their own. I sometimes give patients extra liniment on a cotton ball and place the wet cotton ball into an airtight zip-top bag for them to take home and use later.

POCKET GEMSTONES

I always have a box of small gemstones in my treatment rooms. I let patients pick one that appeals to them, then I read out loud the spiritual and healing significance of the chosen stone from the gemstone reference book in my office. Quite often, the gems closely correlate with the conditions for which the patients are seeking treatment.

I just love how the Universe works through us as practitioners and healing agents like gemstones to give messages to people that lead them to their wellbeing.

Rose quartz, amethyst, blue calcite, hematite, labradorite, malachite, citrine, fluorite, and turquoise are some of my favorites. I also love that this simple act of giving a small crystal to the patient seems to add a sense of magic and miracles back into healthcare, and that patients really do treasure these little gemstones, which actually cost next to nothing.

Positive Affirmation Cards And Calendars

Most of the current thought leaders in personal development have developed decks of cards or calendars with positive affirmations on them. You can make these available in waiting areas, at the reception desk where patients check in and out, or you can have patients pull a random card with you as a way of getting to know them better and building rapport. Louise Hay has a great deck of positive thought cards, and there are also small, micro-sized angel cards that have a one-word affirmation on one side and an image of an angel on the other. I have also found a box of Blessing Cards that contains 210 little cards, each with a single word printed on them—a blessing. You can have your patients pick a blessing before they leave. You might be surprised to see them select cards that coincide perfectly with their current condition, situation, signs, and/or symptoms.

EAR SEEDS

In Chinese medicine, the ear is a map of the body, and we can actually treat the body via the ear. We can insert needles into the auricular acupuncture points, or we can stimulate the points with seeds. Ear seeds do not use needles or puncture the skin and are a great addition to any treatment—chiropractic, massage, physical therapy, acupuncture, or naturopathy.

Traditionally we have used seeds from the Vaccaria plant. However, we now have crystal versions of these seeds available to us from a company called Ear Seeds (www.earseeds.com). They offer all types of ear seeds: the traditional Vaccaria plant, silver beads, gold beads, aromatherapy-infused beads, and even ear seeds that have Swarovski crystals on the outside and sterling silver or 24K gold beads that act as the stimulus for the acupoint on the ear. Their products come with instructions on how to apply the seeds to yourself or your patients. Patients *love* these little treatment enhancements. Plus, they also become a great conversation piece (and free advertisement for you) when your patients get questions and admiration from friends/family about their "ear bling."

With both tangible and nontangible gift-giving ideas, this stop has provided you with a variety of ways to enhance the treatment experience. Each and every suggestion adds value to your treatment session. These unique and health-promoting offerings cost very little but pay us back in two considerable ways: (1) Our patients feel that we offer something that they cannot get from anyone else, and (2) We can be comfortable charging premium prices for the exceptional experience being provided.

As we leave *The Giving Forest*, here are the secrets summarized.

PATIENT SATISFACTION SECRETS FROM THE GIVING FOREST

Intangible

- Hold a space of healing for your patients.

- Express genuine compassion.

- Sit with your patients.

- Massage or anoint your patients' feet.

- Incorporate adjunctive modalities like Healing Touch, Reiki, angel or other oracle-like cards, and so forth.

Tangible

Before, during, and/or after services, offer your patients:

- a cotton ball with aromatherapy on it; you can give additional cotton balls with aromatherapy to patients in tiny zip-top bags.

- health-related and/or calming teas.

- healthy snacks, like single-serving packs of trail mix or fresh fruit.

- licorice sticks in hot water for a sore throat or overall balance.

- chia seeds in small zip-top bags.

- goji berries in hot water and some in a bag to take with them.

- samples of healthy foods that you have prepared in advance.

- at-a-glance calendars to record progress or significant health-related events.

- samples of herbs, supplements, aromatherapy, or other items that you sell in your office.

- gemstones like rose quartz, amethyst, citrine, or blue calcite.

- Little angel cards that have positive affirmations on them.

- ear seeds (natural or crystal versions can be found at www.earseeds.com).

As you can see, small shifts and additions to your patient care can transform an ordinary treatment into an exceptional experience that has the potential to increase patient satisfaction, thereby improving treatment outcomes and bringing more value to your sessions. These are all easy and inexpensive tactics to implement, and they provide significant benefits and rewards. I sincerely hope you have found this information helpful and that it may have stoked or reignited the passionate fire within you to lead others to health, happiness, and well-being.

PART III

The Real Prize Is A Win-Win Outcome

"Physician, heal thyself" is a famous quote from Luke 4:23 in the Bible. Many of us enter the world of healthcare to heal ourselves in the process of learning how to improve the health of others. Many of us need to pay off massive student loans. Many of us want to live a comfortable and abundant life.

This is perfectly normal and absolutely acceptable.

Everything we have been discussing in this book is meant to foster a full circuit of giving and receiving between patient and practitioner. When our patients are happier and get healthier, it makes us feel more pleased and more satisfied with our career choice. When we provide exceptional experiences rather than simple treatments, our patients are willing to pay more for our services because they recognize that we offer much more than the average provider. They win. We win.

CHAPTER 7

Increasing Value Unlocks Wealth

Wanting more money is OK.

Read that again, please. Somewhere deep within the healer archetype resides an all-giving, altruistic, unselfish, almost overly compassionate and egoless character. This may be part of why you are so successful in what you do. However, you deserve all the love, nurturing, fulfillment, joy, and happiness that your treatments, sessions, and healings provide to your patients.

If you:

- Take the time to determine what steps to take to create an extraordinary experience for your patients,

- Take action to incorporate the same into your sessions, and

- Work on yourself to be a clean vessel to channel pure healing,

Then you:

- Stand out as unique and special. Very few healthcare practitioners do this.

- Increase the value of your services by enhancing the experience.

- Deserve to be compensated accordingly for your hard work and dedication to the well-being of your patients.

What good does it do if you help patients prevent surgeries, play golf again, live pain-free, reduce anxiety levels, sleep soundly, and enjoy life to its fullest when you can barely make your car payment each month?

We help people dance again, breathe easier, finally get pregnant, clear up headaches without medication, reduce the need for opioids, and thrive in an almost endless list of other special ways. We bring people to a state of wellness. What is that worth?

Sadly, I often come across practitioners who struggle financially. It doesn't have to be this way. By approaching your practice with the intention of providing your patients with exceptional experiences, you will make your sessions more valuable. You can charge more, and thereby bring more wealth into your own life.

EXPERIENCES ARE WORTH MORE THAN TREATMENTS

My husband and I love to treat ourselves to dinner and what we call "the fancy movies:" Cinépolis. Movie tickets at this chain cost more than double that of mainstream theater. Why are we willing to spend so much? For the experience of sitting back in oversized, insanely comfortable, reclining, couch-like chairs with in-seat food-and-drink service and no more than thirty-six people in each small theater.

I have bought about ten Lady Gaga songs on iTunes. At $0.99 to $1.29 each, that comes to about $13 for all of them together. However, I paid $200 to see her in concert. Why would I do that when I can listen to her songs on repeat all day long? The experience, of course (which was phenomenal).

My brother took his family of four to Disneyland. He paid $900 for all of them to access the Magic Kingdom for one day. That is much more than regular admission. He was willing to spend that much to upgrade to the *MaxPass,* which allows park guests to make reservations for the most popular park attractions, thereby maximizing time enjoying rides and shows—not waiting in lines. He felt this was an experience worth the extra money.

These are just three examples of situations in which creating an exceptional experience results in people being more than willing to pay higher prices. I'm confident you can come up with some cases yourself. The point is, when you add value to your sessions, you make them above average, and you can—and should—charge more.

WORD OF MOUTH CAN GO BOTH WAYS

Question: What do you want to do when you have a great experience? Usual Answer: Tell someone.

Question: What do you want to do when you have a horrible experience? Usual Answer: Tell someone.

Moreover, did you know that an unhappy patient will tell ten people while a happy one will only tell about four or five?[25]

Knowing this further emphasizes the importance of increasing the satisfaction of our patients. If you begin to implement the secrets shared with you during the journey we have taken together in this book, the word-of-mouth marketing circulating about you, your practice, and your treatment experiences will undoubtedly be good ones.

---

[25] Unhappy patients tell more people. See: Tšernov, Kirill. "The Importance of Patient Satisfaction." Qminder, June 21, 2017. https://www.qminder.com/importance-patient-satisfaction/.

CHAPTER 8

The Ongoing Journey:
Stay Aligned With Your Passion

Nurturing sustained enthusiasm and passion for your practice and chosen career is an ongoing effort, not a one-time fix. As with our bodies, so it is with our careers: stagnation can lead to disease. There is a saying: "That which doesn't grow dies."[26] How will you prevent stagnation, prevent career burnout, and continue to expand your skills and better yourself while staying in alignment with what truly brings you joy?

A good way to stay aligned is to continuously remind yourself of the path to which you once committed. Here are two more excerpts from the Hippocratic Oath.

> *May I always act so as to preserve the finest traditions of my calling and may I long experience the joy of healing those who seek my help.*

> *I will remember that there is art to medicine as well as science, and that warmth, sympathy, and understanding may outweigh the surgeon's knife or the chemist's drug.*

---

[26] This quote has been attributed to William S. Burroughs.

A career in healthcare most certainly has peaks and valleys. How will you manage them? Will you listen to your body and soul when they ask for a break and need to be recharged? Will you remove yourself from patient care when you find yourself unable to hold a healing space for patients?

Remember, we may have all the skills and know how to perform all the protocols correctly, but at the end of the day, it will be the overall experience that our patients will remember most and that will have the most impact, be it positive or negative.

Since we know that patient satisfaction is directly tied to your satisfaction, make sure you love what you are doing.

I invite you to live your life in your PJs—
your Passions and Joys.

If you are not passionate about patient care, or if it does not bring you joy, *please* take the time to reconsider how you wish to contribute to healthcare and take any necessary action to get yourself back on a more honest, fulfilling track.

Perhaps you find you are so out of touch with yourself that you don't even know if you are burned out, passionate or not. Here is a good way of answering that question: How do you approach a work day? Do you say, "I get to go to work today," or "I have to go to work today"?

Maybe you do not enjoy direct patient care as you once did, but want to stay in healthcare. Can you bring on an associate to take on some of your patient load? Maybe you are just burned out and need to take a sabbatical to reignite the fire that once burned inside you. Or maybe you are a student who is more than halfway through your program and have come to the realization that you don't really enjoy working with people. *Now* what do you do?

First, there is no reason to panic. You were drawn to medicine and/ or healthcare for a reason. What is that reason? What event(s) took place to lead you to a career in helping others? Look for the clues that have been left for you. There you will find your answer.

This reminds me of a very dear friend of mine, Holly Mead. She was actually a student of mine when I was a teacher in the Master's program for Chinese medicine. At the two-year mark of a four-year program, she realized that while she loved the information she was learning, especially about the Chinese herbs, she did not like treating people with acupuncture. Instead of leaving the program, she surveyed her passions:

She had a passion for:

- Chinese philosophy

- Chinese herbs and formulas
- Business
- Technology
- Animals

So, instead of leaving school, she created one of the first companies that sells Chinese herbs and natural remedies for animals. Within a few short months of being in business, her internet business was making over $10,000 per month while she was still in school. Now, more than ten years later, that business, Paw Healer, is thriving. And my lovely friend Holly is bringing relief, health, and well-being to animals all over the world. And if you think about it, by helping these animals to heal and find relief, she is actually treating humans by bringing peace of mind and comfort to their pet mommies and daddies.

I believe with every fiber of my being that there are endless opportunities for us to participate with and contribute to healthcare. There are so many advances in medicine of which you can be a part. Join a team of researchers working on stem cell therapy. What about telemedicine? Providing life coaching from a medical approach? Biological 3-D printing is gaining momentum: Can you participate there? Maybe you feel called to teach, mentor, or train others? You could create a health-related product, write a book, or go find another way to help others. What is calling to you at this point in time? Only you will know when you find it, because instead of saying things like "I have to…," you will say things like "I get to."

A few years ago, I was talking with a colleague of mine who is a reproductive endocrinologist. She was sharing with me that she had recently brought on an associate to help with her growing practice. She was seeing about fifty patients per week and had about a dozen more on a waitlist. "Oh, wow," I said to her, with an almost anguished look on my face. "Don't you get exhausted by all those women trying to get pregnant?"

"No," she replied. "I love what I do."

That short conversation was incredibly valuable to me and actually helped guide me in my life. At that particular point in time, I was considering engaging in a big marketing campaign to draw more patients to my medium-sized practice, where I was seeing about fifteen to twenty patients per week. My reaction to my colleague allowed me to see a glimpse into my own truth. While seeing fifty patients per week would have exhausted me at that point in my career, it was energizing her. I remember thinking to myself that my reaction in our conversation was total confirmation to me that I needed to keep my practice small and not pursue the marketing campaign. Instead, I took on more teaching rather than more patients.

The clues are there for you. You just have to look for them.

Just like our road trip in this book, now it is time for you to embark on a journey to determine what will lead you to a life where you are enthusiastic, passionate, wealthy, healthy, and thrilled beyond your dreams.

The ideas, suggestions, and methods presented within this book are meant to lead you to double satisfaction—your patients' and yours. You were undoubtedly called to healthcare for a reason. If you have lost your way or do not feel passionate about your career, simply take a pause. Look for all the signs pointing you in the direction of your soul's true desire, purpose and joy (in other words, your *PJs*). They are there, I promise.

St. Catherine of Siena once said:

"Be who God meant you to be and you will set the world on fire."

And an unknown author once wrote:

"Your work is to discover your world and then with all your heart give yourself to it."

May you find your world, stay aligned with your passion, and give yourself whole-heartedly to them both.

With much love and respect to my colleagues in healthcare,

East

APPENDIX A
ACKNOWLEDGMENTS

Henry DeVries, Devin DeVries, and the entire team at Indie Books for guiding me along the path to publishing and helping me to get my information out there.

Alex Tiberi and Giovanni Maciocia, for being some of the early pioneers who brought Chinese medicine to the west while generously sharing their depth and breadth of wisdom and insights with all of us.

Lilian Bridges, who inspired me so greatly that very first time I saw her present at Symposium. I hoped to be like her one day. Lillian delivers the ancient secrets of Chinese medicine with grace and humor.

Dr. Steven Levitt, one of my first teachers, for sharing so much of the unique and special wisdom that was passed down to him from his teachers while acting like a tour guide through the study of Chinese medicine at the Pacific College of Oriental medicine (PCOM) San Diego campus to thousands of students.

Dr. Stacy Gomes and Jack Miller, our bold and courageous leaders at PCOM, for giving me so many opportunities, including but not limited to teaching, presenting at Symposium, creating curriculum, participating in podcasts and distant learning courses.

Some of my favorite teachers of Chinese medicine: Rick Warren, Carol Eliot, and Colleen Timmons, who always made learning Chinese medicine fun, down-to-earth, and applicable in a western world; Marly Wexler, who stressed the importance of organization, working from our hearts, and sitting down with our patients while taking pulses. And Greg Bantick, who taught us how to be mindful and really present with our patients.

Drew Pierson, DAOM, who truly understands the importance of creating an exceptional experience and staying in alignment with passions and joys while blazing new trails for us all in integrative medicine, neurofeedback, and mindfulness.

Elaine Gates Miller, for giving me a chance all those years ago.

Dr. Katharine Kim, DACM, for joining me in my countless endeavors, offering generous assistance, encouragement, and belly-aching laughter along the entire way.

Julie Chang, for keeping me inspired and on track with our many years of mastermind sessions.

Kimberly Allard, my accountability muse and friend who is graciously walking this journey into publishing with me.

My patients, who continue to teach me things about myself and life.

My students, who keep me on my toes and allow me an opportunity to walk my talk and join them on their journey into being providers of healthcare.

My consulting clients, who allow me to be of service and help them reach their highest potentials.

Dr. Jen Campbell, MD, who first shared the term "treat 'em and street 'em" with my doctoral class. She is an inspiration and example of a physician who has beautifully bridged the gap between mainstream and alternative medicines.

Dr. Leena Guptha, DO, MBA, who generously offers her time, energy, insights, wisdom, and information to faculty, students, patients, and the public.

MJ, who provided me with the most exceptional acupuncture treatment experience and continues to do so for countless of others while staying humble about her amazing talents.

For Ellie and Tova Goldschmidt at EarSeeds.com for always bringing such flair to your products, which help so many practitioners provide exceptional experiences for their patients and clients, and for being the absolute best booth neighbors for many years. Your enthusiasm for enhancing experiences with ear seeds while providing effective healing is unmatched.

Sheila Patel, MD, medical director at the Chopra Center, for inviting me to join the Mind-Body Medical Group, allowing me to be of service to the guests and staff.

Victoria Sweet, MD, who publicly endorses the benefits of Chinese medicine while bringing forth some long-forgotten truths about what really makes people heal.

My husband and two children, who gave up time with me so that I could present this information at conferences, workshops, classrooms, and then get it published in a book.

My mother, who I am sure is watching me from heaven with a big smile on her face, as I have followed in her footsteps as a teacher and now author. I love you, Mom.

APPENDIX B

About The Author

East Haradin-Phillips, DAOM, L.Ac., has been a doctor of acupuncture and oriental medicine since 2013, licensed acupuncturist since 1999 and professor of Chinese medicine at the Pacific College of Oriental Medicine since 2004.

With a commitment to helping others actualize their greatest potential and live life in their *PJs* (passions & joys), she continues to help patients, students, other practitioners, and the general public with her lectures, workshops, coaching, and well-being related products. Dr. East currently resides in Del Mar, CA with her husband and two kids.

APPENDIX C

Raise Your Vibration Exercise

Rate how you feel right now on a scale from 1 to 10, with 10 being super enthusiastic, energetic and joyful, 5 being *meh* or *blah,* and 1 not feeling well at all.

Then, sit in a relaxed position and take three deep, cleansing breaths. Close your eyes and think of someone or something for which you have unconditional love. Perhaps it is a parent, a child, a loved one, or a furbaby. Close your eyes and imagine this person or pet and feel all the love you have for them. Think of all the times you have spent together. Imagine this face and observe how good you feel with that image in your mind. (You can even look at a picture.) Sit for the length of time it takes to really feel the love you have for this person or pet. Connect with the feeling of gratitude for having this person or pet in your life. Once you have connected with these feelings, complete your last deep breath by exhaling and opening your eyes.

Now how do you feel? Has your number come up on that 1-to-10 scale?

In most cases, it will improve.

Love is the most powerful force in the Universe and tapping into it can help tremendously at times when we feel that life is beating us down.

APPENDIX D

Hippocratic Oath

I swear to fulfill, to the best of my ability and judgment, this covenant:

I will respect the hard-won scientific gains of those physicians in whose steps I walk, and gladly share such knowledge as is mine with those who are to follow.

I will apply, for the benefit of the sick, all measures [that] are required, avoiding those twin traps of overtreatment and therapeutic nihilism.

I will remember that there is art to medicine as well as science, and that warmth, sympathy, and understanding may outweigh the surgeon's knife or the chemist's drug.

I will not be ashamed to say "I know not," nor will I fail to call in my colleagues when the skills of another are needed for a patient's recovery.

I will respect the privacy of my patients, for their problems are not disclosed to me that the world may know. Most especially must I tread with care in matters of life and death. If it is given me to save a life, all thanks. But it may also be within my power to take a life; this awesome responsibility must be faced with great humbleness and awareness of my own frailty. Above all, I must not play at God.

I will remember that I do not treat a fever chart, a cancerous growth, but a sick human being, whose illness may affect the person's family and economic stability. My responsibility includes these related problems, if I am to care adequately for the sick.

I will prevent disease whenever I can, for prevention is preferable to cure.

I will remember that I remain a member of society, with special obligations to all my fellow human beings, those sound of mind and body as well as the infirm.

If I do not violate this oath, may I enjoy life and art, respected while I live and remembered with affection thereafter. May I always act so as to preserve the finest traditions of my calling and may I long experience the joy of healing those who seek my help.[27]

---

[27] Tyson, Peter. "The Hippocratic Oath Today." PBS. Public Broadcasting Service, March 26, 2001. https://www.pbs.org/wgbh/nova/article/hippocratic-oath-today/.

APPENDIX E

Aromatherapy Recipes

Much of my doctoral research centered around the efficacy of aromatherapy. This powerful healing modality spans time and space and across nearly all cultures. Here are some easy-to-prepare recipes you can use in your practice.

How to Make an Aromatherapy Spray

Get a glass spray bottle, preferably dark glass, like brown, blue, or violet. Do not use plastic, as the essential oils will break down the plastic and contaminate the spray.

General rules of thumb:

1. Add the specific number of drops of oils to an empty 2-oz bottle.

2. Add 1/3 oz. alcohol or vegetable glycerin which will act as a solvent.

3. Fill bottle with distilled or spring water and shake well.

Notes: Some people think that distilled water is ideal, as it doesn't contain molecules that may clog sprayers. I prefer spring water because I believe it is more alive and full of energy than distilled. Oil and water don't naturally mix. This means you will need to shake the bottles very well to get the oils and water to combine or add a solvent. For solvent, add approximately 1/3 ounce (10 ml) of alcohol or vegetable glycerin to the aromatherapy spray. Vodka works well as a non-odorous alcohol solvent.

Pain Relief

2 oz. (50 ml) spring or distilled water solution (solvent included)

4 drops peppermint

6 drops lavender

1 drop spearmint

1–2 drops sandalwood

Calming

2 (50 ml) spring or distilled water solution (solvent included)

2 drops vetiver

1–2 drops sandalwood

2 drops geranium

2 drops lavender

1 drop Helichrysum

2 drops Roman chamomile

Immunity

2 (50 ml) spring or distilled water solution (solvent included)

4 drops frankincense

8 drops eucalyptus

4 drops lemon

2 drops lavender

How to use the sprays:

- Spray them on your hands before you work with, or touch, your patients. The essential oils in the sprays are antimicrobial and will refresh your hands while also giving aromatherapy to your patient.

- Spray your treatment space.

- Spray three times onto a cotton ball and have the patient smell the saturated cotton ball.

The Experience Quotient

Read each line item and score yourself based on the scale provided	Never Rarely 0	Some-times 1	About 50% of the time 2	Almost Always 3	Always 4
Golden Circle					
I offer warm and genuine invitations to be treated when attending social or networking events or even just meeting people in public.					
Scheduling an appointment is easy and immediate, allowing people to schedule at their convenience at various times.					
I honor timeliness: I begin and end sessions on time.					
I clearly define expectations and obtain agreement over same with patients.					
I involve family members, caretakers and/or loved ones with big decisions and/or treatment plans.					
I follow up throughout the treatment plan cycle to monitor compliance and provide support.					
I follow up after treatment plan cycle(s) and stay connected with patients.					
I engage in patient care co-management by working with other practitioners where and when it is necessary or appropriate.					
Healing Temple					
My practice location is easy to find and access, within a safe environment and not situated next to conflicting types of businesses.					
There is adequate, if not ample, parking available to patients at my location(s).					
The reception and waiting areas have a warm and welcoming ambiance.					
All spaces within the office are clear of any clutter including rooms only accessed by myself and my staff.					

All treatment spaces feel warm, comfortable and soothing.					
I practice being my own patient by periodically sampling my equipment, products, and/or music.					
Music and/or aromatherapy is offered to my patients.					
The Great Sage					
I LOVE what I do and feel in full alignment with myself, my purpose and my passion.					
I am a positive role model for my patients, I walk my talk.					
The words I use with my patients are positive, encouraging compassionate and uplifting.					
I hold a healing space for my patients, seeing them as well, healed and complete rather than a certain condition, symptom or diagnosis.					
I practice self-care regularly and preventatively while maintaining a healthy work-life balance.					
The Giving Forest					
I take the time to sit with my patients.					
I am genuinely present with my patients, engaging in eye contact and practicing mindfulness.					
I incorporate adjunctive modalities into my treatment sessions (i.e., Reiki, healing hands, intuition, sound healing).					
I offer water, tea, and/or small snacks for my patients.					
I offer education materials like handouts, videos, resources, and/or website links.					
Add up all your scores: *Best possible score is 100 points.*					

APPENDIX G

Works Referenced

Anderson, Roger T, Fabian T Camacho, and Rajesh Balkrishnan. "Willing to Wait?: The Influence of Patient Wait Time on Satisfaction with Primary Care." *BMC Health Services Research*, 7:31 (2007). https://doi.org/10.1186/1472-6963-7-31.

Baldwin, Ann Linda, Christina Wagers, and Gary E Schwartz. "Reiki Improves Heart Rate Homeostasis in Laboratory Rats." *The Journal of Alternative and Complementary Medicine* (New York, N.Y.). U.S. National Library of Medicine, May 2008. https://www.ncbi.nlm.nih.gov/pubmed/18435597.

Bogner, Jennifer, Erinn M Hade, Juan Peng, Cynthia L Beaulieu, Susan D Horn, John D Corrigan, Flora M Hammond, et al. "Family Involvement in Traumatic Brain Injury Inpatient Rehabilitation: A Propensity Score Analysis of Effects on Outcomes During the First Year After Discharge." Archives of physical medicine and rehabilitation. U.S. National Library of Medicine, May 9, 2019. https://www.ncbi.nlm.nih.gov/pubmed/31077646.

Carter, Sherrie Bourg. "Why Mess Causes Stress: 8 Reasons, 8 Remedies." *Psychology Today*. Sussex Publishers. Accessed June 21, 2019. https://www.psychologytoday.com/us/

blog/high-octane-women/201203/why-mess-causes-stress-8-reasons-8-remedies.

Charnock, Colin. "Swabbing of Waiting Room Magazines Reveals Only Low Levels of Bacterial Contamination." The British journal of general practice : the journal of the Royal College of General Practitioners. Oxford University Press, January 1, 2005. https://www.ncbi.nlm.nih.gov/pmc/articles/PMC1266241/.

Daniali, Hojjat, and Magne Arve Flaten. "A Qualitative Systematic Review of Effects of Provider Characteristics and Nonverbal Behavior on Pain, and Placebo and Nocebo Effects." Frontiers in psychiatry. Frontiers Media S.A., April 15, 2019. https://www.ncbi.nlm.nih.gov/pubmed/31037059.

Drake, Crystal R., H. Russell Searight, and Kristina Olson-Pupek. "The Influence of Art-Making on Negative Mood States in University Students." *American Journal of Applied Psychology*. Science and Education Publishing, January 23, 2014. http://pubs.sciepub.com/ajap/2/3/3/.

Evolution, Collective. "Neuroscientists Discover A Song That Reduces Anxiety By 65 Percent (Listen)." *Collective Evolution*, May 22, 2018. https://www.collective-evolution.com/2016/12/25/neuroscientists-discover-a-song-that-reduces-anxiety-by-65-percent-listen/.

Haradin, East. "Combining Acupuncture with Aromatherapy to Enhance the Treatment of Stress." *Meridians Journal of Acupuncture and Oriental Medicine*, 2018. https://www.meridiansjaom.com/vol-6-no-2-abstracts.html.

Hojat, Mohammadreza, Daniel Z Louis, Fred W Markham, Richard Wender, Carol Rabinowitz, and Joseph S Gonnella. "Physicians' Empathy and Clinical Outcomes for Diabetic Patients." Academic medicine : journal of the Association of American Medical Colleges. U.S. National Library of Medicine, March 2011. https://www.ncbi.nlm.nih.gov/pubmed/21248604.

Huang, Hsiang-Ling, Swee-Ling Lim, Lu Kuan-Hung, and Lee-Yan Sheen. "Antidepressant-like Effects of Gan-Mai-Dazao-Tang via Monoamine Regulatory Pathways on Forced Swimming Test in Rats." Journal of Traditional and Complementary Medicine. Elsevier, March 3, 2017. https://www.sciencedirect.com/science/article/pii/S2225411017300123.

Iwamoto, Yuko, and Minoru Hoshiyama. "Alteration of Time Perception in Young and Elderly People during Jigsaw Puzzle Tasks with Different Complexities." Occupational Therapy International 18, no. 4 (2011): 194–200. https://doi.org/10.1002/oti.322.

Last, Nicole, Emily Tufts, and Leslie E Auger. "The Effects of Meditation on Grey Matter Atrophy and Neurodegeneration: A Systematic Review." Journal of Alzheimer's Disease: JAD. U.S. National Library of Medicine, 2017. https://www.ncbi.nlm.nih.gov/pubmed/27983555.

Mackay, Nicola, Stig Hansen, and Oona McFarlane. "Autonomic Nervous System Changes during Reiki Treatment: a Preliminary Study." Journal of Alternative and Complementary Medicine (New York, N.Y.). U.S. National

Library of Medicine, December 2004. https://www.ncbi.
nlm.nih.gov/pubmed/15674004/.

Manary, Matthew P., William Boulding, Richard Staelin, and
Seth W. Glickman. "The Patient Experience and Health
Outcomes." *New England Journal of Medicine* 368, no. 3
(2013): 201–3. https://doi.org/10.1056/nejmp1211775.

Myers, Katie L. Florida State University Thesis: "The Use of Patient-
Preferred Music to Improve Patient Experience during
Interfacility Ambulance Transport." September, 2013.
https://fsu.digital.flvc.org/islandora/object/fsu:185145/
datastream/PDF/view

Nautiyal, Chandra Shekhar, Puneet Singh Chauhan, and Yeshwant
Laxman Nene. "Medicinal Smoke Reduces Airborne
Bacteria." *Journal of Ethnopharmacology* 114, no. 3 (2007):
446–51. https://doi.org/10.1016/j.jep.2007.08.038.

Prakash, Bhanu. "Patient Satisfaction." *Journal of Cutaneous
and Aesthetic Surgery* 3, no. 3 (2010): 151. https://doi.
org/10.4103/0974-2077.74491.

Shin, Byung-Cheul, and Myeong Soo Lee. "Effects of Aromatherapy Acupressure on Hemiplegic Shoulder Pain And
Motor Power in Stroke Patients: A Pilot Study." *The Journal
of Alternative and Complementary Medicine* 13, no. 2 (2007):
247–52. https://doi.org/10.1089/acm.2006.6189.

Sidra Ishaque, Taimur Saleem, and Waris Qidwai. "Knowledge,
Attitudes and Practices Regarding Gemstone Therapeutics
in a Selected Adult Population in Pakistan." *BMC
Complementary and Alternative Medicine*. BioMed Central,

August 26, 2009. https://doi.org/10.1186/1472-6882-9-32.

Swayden, Kelli J, Karen K Anderson, Lynne M Connelly, Jennifer S Moran, Joan K McMahon, and Paul M Arnold. "Effect of Sitting vs. Standing on Perception of Provider Time at Bedside: a Pilot Study." *Patient Education and Counseling.* U.S. National Library of Medicine, February 2012. https://www.ncbi.nlm.nih.gov/pubmed/21719234.

Tyson, Peter. "The Hippocratic Oath Today." PBS. Public Broadcasting Service, March 26, 2001. https://www.pbs.org/wgbh/nova/article/hippocratic-oath-today/.

Tšernov, Kirill. "The Importance of Patient Satisfaction." Qminder. Qminder, June 21, 2017. https://www.qminder.com/importance-patient-satisfaction/.

Wilkinson, Dawn S., Pamela L. Chatman, James E. Johnson, Terrance L. Barbour, Nilufer Barbour, Yvonne Myles, and Antonio Reel. "The Clinical Effectiveness of Healing Touch." *The Journal of Alternative and Complementary Medicine*, Vol. 8, No. 1, 2004. https://www.liebertpub.com/doi/abs.

www.ingramcontent.com/pod-product-compliance
Lightning Source LLC
Chambersburg PA
CBHW031945190326
41519CB00007B/663